PINK GOLDFISH

DEFY NORMAL, EXPLOIT IMPERFECTION AND CAPTIVATE YOUR CUSTOMERS

Stan Phelps
&
David Rendall

D1501682

Published by 9 INCH Marketing

Copy Editing by Lee Heinrich of Write Way Publishing Company
Layout by Evan Carroll

ISBN: 978-0-9849838-9-6

First Printing: 2018
Printed in the United States of America

Pink Goldfish is available for bulk orders. For further details and special pricing, please e-mail stan@purplegoldfish.com or call +1.919.360.4702.

This book is dedicated to my youngest son, James Phelps.
Your weaknesses hold the keys to your strengths. Never stop
embracing what makes you unique and special.

—Stan Phelps

This book is dedicated to my parents, Vernon and Shary,
and my grandparents, Leland and Ruby.

—David Rendall

ACKNOWLEDGMENTS

We'd like to thank everyone who inspired us, supported us, or provided feedback for this book:

Arif Abdulla, Karen Albritton, Jamie Anderson, Matt Anderson, Kenneth Anum, Ben Baker, Ben Baldanza, Marilynn Barber, Brent Barbour, Andrew Barton, Brady Bell, Jeff Bezos, Josh Bledsoe, Laszlo Bock, Alex Bogusky, Jake Bohall, Richard Branson, Troyen A. Brennan, Martyn Brewer, Jared Brickman, Bo Burlingham, Skip Carney, Evan Carroll, S. Truett Cathy, Dorie Clark, Marty Cobb, Steve Cody, Josh Coffy, Ben Cohen, Sandy Colon, Scott Cook, Julian Cromer, Ted Curtin, Elisa Daalder, Dietmar Dahman, Ray Dalio, Alec Dalton, Kironmoy Datta, Adam DeSantis, Dennis Devlin, Minter Dial, Brian Doyle, Frank Druffel, Johnny Earle, Jason Falls, Robert Ferguson, Veronica (Niki) Fielding, John Fluevog, Christopher Fuller, Lance Gibbs, Stacey Gipson, Greg Glassman, Cody Goldberg, WL Gore, Keith Green, Sean-Michael Green, Lewis Greenberg, Shaun Griffith, Chris Guillebeau, David Hadden, Chad Hahn, Steven Handmaker, Phil Hansen, Chip Heath, Dan Heath, Lee Heinrich, Michelle Hill, Tony Hsieh, Jackie Huba, Jony Ive, Rick Jarrett, Steve Jobs, Emily Juhnke, Shawn Kanungo, Max Kampenaar, Russ Klein, Ashley Knepper, Takeru Kobayashi, Kristin Kohler Burrows, Azhar Laher, Lazarus Lake, Judy Lahner, Jim Lawenda, Tim League, Michelle LeBlanc, Tammy Lenski, Rick Liebling, Lisa Lindstrom, John Mackey, Mike Maddock, Elizabeth Magill, Chris Malone, Sharon Delaney McCloud, Madi McDougald, Lauren McGhee, Dr. Gary McGrath, Steve McDonald, Suzanne Miglucci, Rebecca Minkoff, Michelle Miracle, Youngme Moon, Jerry Murrell, Sumner Musolf, Drew Neisser, Martha O'Gorman, Michael O'Leary, Theresa Pantazopoulos, Tom Peters, Jennifer Phelps, Dan Pink, Jeff Pocklington, Andy Puzder, Anna Rendall,

Emma Rendall, Sophia Rendall, Stephanie Rendall, Cory Richardson, Danny Rosin, Paige Sandhu, Karl Sakas, Kimberly Schubeck, Bhupesh Shah, Herbert Sherman, Brittany Silva, Spencer Silver, Mary Sikorski, Jeff Sommers, Earl Springer, Melissa St. John, Rajan Tata, Beth Thuin, Lynsi Torres, Jimmy Vee, Becky Vucksta, Ruth Graves Wakefield, Red Wassenich, Alyssa Waxenberg, Jenn Wheeler, Hayley Woodin, and Misty Young.

CONTENTS

FOREWORD

BY MIKE MADDOCK

"It ain't what you don't know that gets you into trouble.
It's what you know for sure that just ain't so."

- Mark Twain

Thank God, the nuns were wrong.

"Doodling is not what good students do." This was the lesson that I was taught but never learned at the ripe age of twelve. I was attending St. Joseph's Catholic School in Homewood, Illinois, and the good sisters were trying to give my parents their money's worth. Sister Helen, trying to set me straight, had just slapped me with yet another detention in her effort to teach me that daydreaming and doodling were not ways to get ahead in the world.

Lucky for me, I was apparently slower than the rest of the kids.

It wasn't until twelve years later, when the *Pioneer Press* in Minneapolis offered me a job as an editorial cartoonist, that I realized that the good sister was incorrect in her assertion. The recalibrated lesson was amplified when I attempted to resign from my job as an Art Director at a small packaging firm in Illinois to pursue my new career as a cartoonist. My boss promised to double my salary if I stayed on, saying that my ability to blend headlines and images was rare and critical to the firm.

I decided to stay, smiling at the heavens on the way out the door.

"Talking in class is not what good students do." This second lesson was impressed upon me...well, from as early as I can remember. My gift for gab was legendary in my family and at school, so needless to say, it came up more than occasionally in parent-teacher conferences. Today I am convinced that I would have spent more time in detention for talking but the nuns knew they simply couldn't get me to shut up, so they just dinged me on my report card instead.

I was asked to keynote a conference in Las Vegas last year. I was paid more than I made in my first year of work out of college. I shared the stage with President Clinton, President Bush, plus a host of best-selling authors and world-renowned thought leaders. I got to open the conference and exit the stage to a standing ovation—it was absolutely epic. As I waved at the audience, I was thinking of the nuns who spent years trying to get me to shut up.

Hallelujah! Turns out that gabby students make good public speakers. Who knew?

This leads me to my buddies David Rendall and Stan Phelps. I have a very strong suspicion that they both spent some quality time in detention because of their refusal to conform. Lucky us.

David and Stan will tell you things you need to know. Things like: what makes you weak, makes you strong and being different is what makes you outstanding. They are both experts at distilling uniqueness in business. They'll challenge you to accept your flaws and turn them into an unfair competitive advantage in business and in life.

Coach John Wooden said, "Show me your friends and I'll show you your future." I am pleased to say that a couple of my super-smart friends are pink. Enjoy the book.

INTRODUCTION

BY STAN PHELPS

*"The search for meaningful distinction is central to
the marketing effort. If marketing is about anything,
it is about achieving customer-getting distinction
by differentiating what you do and how you operate.
All else is derivative of that and only that."*
- Ted Levitt

Most florists sell beautiful, living flowers that smell wonderful. Most people send flowers in an attempt to communicate love or affection. They want to please the person who receives the flowers.

But what if you just had a bad breakup? What if you have enemies but you're not quite ready to hire a hitman? Dirty Rotten Flowers[1] is for you. This business sends bouquets of dead, rotting flowers to your not-so-loved ones.

Dirty Rotten Flowers is a great example of a pink goldfish. They differentiate by being bad at seemingly essential parts of the flower business. They offer dirty, instead of beautiful. They offer rotten, instead of fresh. They found weirdness in weakness. Their flaws make them awesome. They're just one of over 250 companies we've researched for this book. Buckle up, there are many more examples to come. We've been collecting them for a while...

---

1. http://www.businessnewsdaily.com/8755-strange-businesses.html

BACKSTORY ON COLLECTING

I once heard on NPR that the most impactful time in your life is when you are twenty-two years old. The circumstances and experiences around that year will have a huge influence on your future. For me, it became a harbinger for this book.

I turned twenty-two just after my college graduation and celebrated my birthday in London. I had received a Blue Card to work in England. The program called BUNAC allowed students or recent graduates the opportunity to work for six months in Great Britain. Needing to find a flat in London, I met two recent NC State grads named Kent Lovett and Parke Morris. Together we found a place in central London. It was a one bedroom flat with three beds in Mayfair. The apartment was on White Horse Street near Shepherd's Market. It was centrally located just off Piccadilly in the West End. Soon after moving in, Parke received a job up north in Sheffield. He was replaced by David Ackerman, a fellow BUNACer from New York City and a recent graduate of NYU.

Photo Credit: Kent Lovett, Pictured - Stan Phelps (right) and David Ackerman (left) on the corner of Piccadilly & White Horse

One of the many quirky things we did in our flat was to create a collage on our kitchen wall. It was a colorful assortment of cards. The technical name for these cards was tart cards. Not familiar with tart cards? Here's an explanation of the phenomenon according to Wikipedia[2]

> The cards originated in the 1960s in places such as Soho, London, as handwritten postcards. As direct references to prostitution would generally be unacceptable, the cards were carefully worded and often contained euphemistic references to sex.... By the late 1980s they had become black-and-white photocopied cards containing printed text and telephone numbers. In larger cities, cards began to be placed in phone boxes. Over time they have become regarded as items of "accidental art" and developed a cult following. They have influenced the work of mainstream artists, inspiring collections, research, exhibitions, and books.

Photo Credit: Wikipedia Commons

It started small. The rules of collecting were simple. No duplicates could be posted on the wall. Every so often we would make trips on the Underground to visit different parts of London to bolster our

2. https://en.wikipedia.org/wiki/Tart_card

growing collection. After a few months, we had amassed nearly 500 cards. Each card was unique, different in its own way.

Photo Credit: Kent Lovett, Pictured - Stan Phelps (left) and David Ackerman (right) sitting in our kitchen at 8 White Horse Street

The colors, taglines, and calls to action were fascinating. To say it was an education would be an understatement. We learned a bunch of interesting acronyms. Some of the sayings were kitschy, and we each had our personal favorites. We would challenge each other to finish a saying by providing only the first word or words. Some of the notorious cards included,

"PVC... for you and me"

"Roses are red, violets are blue... Christmas is coming and so may you"

"I've been naughty... I need a good panky"

It was a study in design and subtle advertising copy. Some of the clever calls to action were *"large chest for sale"* or *"French Lessons."* The importance of differentiating with your copy was key. To stand out you needed to push boundaries and embrace a little weirdness. In some instances, it was a matter of simplicity or subtracting to get to the essence. My favorite was one of the shorter sayings that got right to the benefit.

Photo Credit: Kent Lovett, Pictured - a collage on our kitchen wall at 8 White Horse Street

This act of collecting would leave a lasting impression. Seeking out differentiation and collecting examples would become hallmarks of the Goldfish series of books nearly two decades later.

FLAUNTING WEIRDNESS

This last story about collecting tart cards is potentially offensive to some people. In the spirit of this book, I've leaned in against my own instinct to take it out. I've kept it in because it is different. Differentiation at its core is about being weird, bad, and weaker than the norm. In the same vein, this example from Spirit Airlines demonstrates that this can be a useful corporate tactic.

Embracing innuendo and being controversial have become hallmarks of Spirit Airlines, the Florida-based company that bills itself as the country's first "ultralow-fare" airline. Spirit is known for loud ad campaigns with sexual innuendo, ads in passenger cabins and on flight attendants' aprons, and, most of all, very cheap airfares. Here are some recent advertisements with references to wieners, M.I.L.F.s, and balls:

SEARCHING FOR DIFFERENTIATION

I began my writing over a decade ago with a blog called 9 INCH marketing. Nothing personal I assure you. The nine inches are a reference to the average distance between the stem of your brain and the top of your heart. I believe making the journey from the brain to the heart of your customer is the longest and hardest nine inches in marketing. Over the course of that first year, I blogged about fifty different marketing-related topics.

I was searching for what I thought would be a game changer in marketing and business. In 2009, I experienced a "moment of truth" in New York City that changed my life and focus. It was a summer evening, and I was with a work colleague. Brad and I were at a trendy rooftop bar. One of those places in Manhattan where a bottle of beer is $15. We were waiting to meet a few people before heading over to a networking event. I noticed an older gentleman sitting on his own across from us. As the minutes passed, it became obvious that he was waiting for someone. After half an hour passed, I decided to strike up a conversation. I leaned in and jokingly asked, "Do you know that we spend 10 percent of our life waiting?" I assured him I knew this was true because I once had read it on the internet. We laughed and then started talking about the etiquette of waiting. I stressed the importance of being on time. Right then the old man shook his head and said something I'll never forget. "There is no such thing as being on time. In fact, being on time is a myth," he said. Wait a second, I thought. I've been on time before. He waved his finger at me and asserted, "No. Being on time is a fallacy. In life, you are either early...or you are late. No one is ever on time."

This was a complete paradigm shift for me. I went home that night and starting thinking about how this applies in business. My mind immediately linked this to marketing and meeting customer expectations. I've always thought that the idea of simply meeting expectations was a surefire recipe for disaster. It almost guarantees you will fall short. I walked away from that brief conversation with a new conviction. Too much attention was being placed on awareness and acquisition in marketing. I believed that successful businesses would need to find the little things to maximize the customer experience by putting customers first. Taking care of the customers they had, in other words, so those customers would bring them the (referred) customers they wanted.

I became a disciple of the late Ted Levitt. Levitt, a former Harvard Business School professor, believed that businesses should put the customer at the center of everything they do. Levitt asserted, "The search for meaningful distinction is central to the marketing effort. If marketing is about anything, it is about achieving customer-getting distinction by differentiating what you do and how you operate. All else is derivative of that and only that." I believed the focus of business should be on customers and not just chasing bottom line profits. Profit was the result, not the aim. I believed customer experience was the route to competitive differentiation and would soon become the new marketing. This book focuses on customer-getting distinction via differentiation.

A SERIES IS BORN

After collecting over 1,001 examples and writing my first book, *Purple Goldfish*, my thinking was slightly altered. I found that the companies who did the little extras for customers also applied the same principles for their employees. In fact, many of those successful companies seemed to place a greater emphasis on culture and putting their employees first to create competitive differentiation.

It led me to crowdsource another thousand examples. These examples were focused on the little things for employees to help drive engagement and reinforce culture. The result was my second book, *Green Goldfish*.

My outlook after *Green Goldfish* evolved once again. I had previously held the view that you should treat all your customers and all your employees the same. I came to realize that for most companies, 80 percent of profitability is created by just 20 percent of customers. In addition, 80 percent of the value that is created by a business comes from just 20 percent of the employees. I realized that you should not treat everyone the same; you should treat everyone fairly. My third book in the original trilogy is called *Golden Goldfish*. Gold focuses on the little things you do for your *"vital few"* customers and employees in business.

The fourth book in the Goldfish series is *Blue Goldfish,* co-authored with Evan Carroll. Blue focuses on how to leverage technology, data, and analytics to create both prophets and profits. It examines the 3R's of relationship, responsiveness, and readiness. It was followed by *Red Goldfish*, co-authored with Graeme Newell. *Red Goldfish* examines how purpose is becoming the ultimate differentiator in business. It explores how business is evolving, the importance of putting purpose first, how to define your purpose, the eight purpose archetypes, and how to create the little things that bring purpose to life.

MEETING DAVID

David and I met at a networking event in Cary, North Carolina, hosted by Dr. Kevin C. Snyder. David was hard to miss in the room. Beyond his 6'6" height, David was wearing pink pants and pink sneakers. That night I learned about *Freak Factor*. This seminal book outlines a simple premise—what makes us weird makes us wonderful and what makes us weak can also be what makes us strong. In the words of Daniel Pink, "David Rendall has a radical prescription for chronic dissatisfaction: Stop working on your weaknesses and start amplifying them instead. The *Freak Factor* flips the cult of self-improvement on its head with stories of real people who have soared to success by embracing their uniqueness." The principles in *Freak Factor* have universal application. They can be applied to personal development, leadership, parenting, and relationships. I immediately saw the power of the principles and how they applied to business.

COMPETING ON DIFFERENTIATION

In her book *Different - Escaping the Competitive Herd*, Harvard Business School marketing professor Youngme Moon argues that "the ability to compete is dependent upon the ability to differentiate from competitors." However, she goes on to say, "The number of companies who are truly able to achieve competitive separation is depressingly small." This is because companies tend to define their strengths and weaknesses using the same measurements and standards as their competitors. This leads to homogeneity, not differentiation. When everyone is trying to build on the same strengths and eliminate the same weaknesses, all companies start to look the same. So how can you create one of the few organizations that become extraordinary? How can you succeed where most organizations fail? Building on differentiation is the aim of *Pink Goldfish*.

This book is broken into three sections:

Section I outlines the **Why**. It explores the need to embrace weirdness and amplify weakness to differentiate in business. We reveal how everything we've learned about weakness is wrong. We'll show how every weakness has a corresponding strength. We examine the seven reasons to embrace weirdness. The section ends with an explanation of our metaphor of the pink goldfish where we'll share the symbolism of the goldfish and the reasoning behind the color pink.

Section II showcases the **What**. We'll examine the concept of being F.L.A.W.S.O.M. This is the idea of embracing your flaws. You can succeed because of your flaws, not despite of them. We use F.L.A.W.S.O.M. as our acronym for the seven types of pink goldfish. We share our flaunting matrix and each pink type: **F**launting, **L**opsiding, **A**ntagonizing, **W**ithholding, **S**werving, **O**pposing, and **M**icro-weirding. This section points out the ways to stand out by doing more of what makes you weird and less of what makes you normal in business.

Section III explains the **How**. Here we share the process of finding your own pink goldfish. We delve into the four A's. The first A is assess, and it involves understanding what makes you weird or weak. The second A is appreciate. Appreciation is accepting and taking ownership of your uniqueness. The third A is amplify. Amplification is the process of turning up the dial to bring your differentiation to life. The final A is align. Aligning involves looking at those areas of weirdness and weakness that resonate with your customer and create meaningful differentiation.

Ready to jump in? We'll start with a new perspective on organizational strengths and weaknesses. Let's go...

SECTION I

OVERVIEW
(THE WHY)

CHAPTER 1

WHY WEAKNESS?

*"We are led to truth by our weaknesses
as well as our strengths."*

- Parker Palmer

Everything we've learned about weakness is wrong. Our parents, teachers, and managers taught us that we need to find and fix our flaws in order to be successful in life and business. There are four parts to this belief system.

First, we believe that to be successful we need to be normal, fit in, and not stand out. This means that we should follow the herd. Second, we think we should be fixing weaknesses and improving flaws in our companies. We believe that well-rounded and well-balanced companies are the ones that win. Third, we're convinced that our company could be great at everything if we are diligent enough. Similarly, we think we could make everyone happy if we try hard enough. Finally, we believe that we could stand out if we just have enough discipline and perseverance.

All of these beliefs seem empowering, but they are actually debilitating. They tell us that we have the potential to succeed, but they mislead us as to where that potential lies and how we should apply that potential. These beliefs lead to companies defining their strengths and weaknesses using the same measurements and standards as their competitors.

This book offers four competing beliefs:

First, fitting in and becoming a "me too" brand will never lead to success. Benchmarking is not the path to greatness. Second, trying to fix a weakness is a waste of time and effort. Third, if you try to be great at everything, you will end up being great at nothing. If you try to please everyone, you won't end up pleasing anyone. This is a recipe for mediocrity. Fourth, discipline and perseverance are finite but renewable resources. We have to be efficient in how and when we choose to use them.

We believe that it is good to be different, to stick out and be unique. We believe that it is good to flaunt your weaknesses instead of fixing them. It is good to be unbalanced. We believe that the flaws of a brand can make it awesome.

This may well seem like a ridiculous argument. If you're skeptical, that's okay. You should be. We'll spend the rest of the book proving the value of exploiting flaws. Now, let's talk about weirdness...

CHAPTER 2

WHY WEIRDNESS?

"Conformity is the ruin of the mind."

- Jesse Shelley

HERE ARE SEVEN REASONS THAT WEIRD WORKS:

1. BEING WEIRD MAKES YOU RARE...BEING NORMAL MAKES YOU ORDINARY.

Scarcity increases value. Diamonds are valuable primarily because they are rare. Sand and salt are far less valuable, not because they aren't useful, but because they are so ordinary and plentiful.

2. BEING WEIRD MAKES YOU ORIGINAL...BEING NORMAL MAKES YOU EASY TO IMITATE.

Keith Ferrazzi, in his book *Never Eat Alone*, argues that we must "be distinct or be extinct.... The best brands, like the most interesting people, have a distinct message.... When it comes to making an impression, differentiation is the name of the game. Confound expectation. Shake it up."

The value of any product or service immediately decreases once there are acceptable alternatives. An obvious example comes from the world of work. When someone's job can be done faster or cheaper by a computer or an outsourced contractor in another location, that job becomes less valuable. The salary for that position decreases and the likelihood of being replaced increases.

Original brands avoid imitation. They make it difficult to be replaced. There are no good substitutes.

3. BEING WEIRD MAKES YOU NOTICEABLE...BEING NORMAL MAKES YOU INVISIBLE.

Fitting in and following the herd makes us invisible. If we do things well, no one can see us. If our business fits in, everyone drives right by. No one stops. They don't know we're even there. If they do stop, they don't stay long, and they don't buy anything because our products or services are just like everyone else's. If we fit in, we don't get any attention. And attention is one of the most valuable gifts we can get from customers.

4. BEING WEIRD MAKES YOU SURPRISING...BEING NORMAL MAKES YOU PREDICTABLE.

As Chip and Dan Heath explain in *Made to Stick*, we are more likely to be persuaded by messages that are unexpected. If we can surprise someone, we create an emotional response. Our brain is programmed to release dopamine as part of an emotional response. Dopamine is literally the Post-it note for our memory. Surprising and ultimately delighting a customer generates experiences that are remembered and shared with others.

5. BEING WEIRD MAKES YOU MEMORABLE...BEING NORMAL MAKES YOU FORGETTABLE.

We remember the unusual events in our lives, not the common ones. If no one remembers your brand message, then you don't have the opportunity to influence them. The worst criticism that Simon Cowell, the caustic judge of *American Idol*, can give is that a contestant is forgettable. In contrast, one of his most powerful compliments is that a contestant is memorable. He recently told one female singer, "You are such a strange person. I mean that as a compliment." We remember people and businesses that are strange.

6. BEING WEIRD MAKES YOU REMARKABLE...NOR-MAL GIVES PEOPLE NOTHING TO TALK ABOUT.

When we see something different, we want to tell other people about it. Once people remember your business, the biggest challenge is getting them to tell others about you. As Mark Sanborn demonstrated in *The Fred Factor*, a story about his extraordinary mailman, if you are remarkable enough, someone might even write a book about you. Word of mouth is powerful for both individuals and businesses.

7. BEING WEIRD MAKES YOU INFLUENTIAL...BEING NORMAL MAKES YOU POWERLESS.

If other people are sharing your message, it increases your influence because it enables your message to reach a larger audience.

A lot of people pay lip service to the value of being different and standing out. Many believe it's an essential part of any marketing strategy. However, it is difficult to be different. When you try to be different, there will be pressure to fit in.

Robert Quinn argues in *Deep Change* that "deviance will always generate external pressures to conform." Some people see deviance as wrong and dangerous, so they respond with disdain and mockery. That is why E. E. Cummings warned, "It takes courage to grow up and turn out to be who you really are." It can be risky to stick out. Because of this, we tend to give up on being truly different. Instead, we just do what the competition is doing.

However, it can be just as dangerous to simply remain average. Management guru Tom Peters argues that it is no longer safe to be the same, to be normal, to be indistinct. Let that sink in for a minute. He is saying that the only safe move—only prudent choice, the only wise decision—is to become unusual, different, strange, and remarkable. We wholeheartedly agree. This book is based on the belief that weird brands win.

Now let's explore the metaphors behind the pink goldfish...

CHAPTER 3

WHY A GOLDFISH?

"Big doors swing on little hinges"

- W. Clement Stone

The origin of the goldfish dates back to 2009. It has become a signature part of this book series. *Pink Goldfish* is the sixth color in the series. The goldfish represents something small, but despite its size, something with the ability to make a big difference.

The first part of the inspiration for the goldfish came from Kimpton Hotels. The boutique hotel chain introduced something new in 2001. The Hotel Monaco began to offer travelers the opportunity to adopt a temporary travel companion for their stay. Perhaps you were traveling on business and getting a little lonely. Or maybe you were with family and missing your family pet. Kimpton to the rescue; they gave you a goldfish for your stay. They called the program Guppy Love.

"The 'Guppy Love' program is a fun extension of our pet-friendly nature as well as our emphasis on indulging the senses to heighten the travel experience," said Steve Pinetti, Senior Vice President of Sales & Marketing for Kimpton Hotels and Restaurants, of which Hotel Monaco is part of their premier collection. "Everything about Hotel Monaco appeals directly to the senses, and 'Guppy Love' offers one more unique way to relax, indulge and promote health of mind, body and spirit in our home-away-from-home atmosphere."

The second part of our goldfish inspiration came from the peculiar growth of a goldfish. The average common goldfish is between three to four inches in length (ten centimeters), yet the largest in the world is almost six times that size! For comparison, imagine walking down the street and bumping into someone who's three stories tall.

How can there be such a disparity between regular goldfish and their monster cousins? Well, it turns out that the growth of the goldfish is determined by five factors. Just like goldfish, not all businesses grow equally, and we believe that the growth of a product or service faces the same five factors that affect the growth of a goldfish.

1. SIZE OF THE ENVIRONMENT = THE MARKET

GROWTH FACTOR: The size of the bowl or pond.

IMPACT: Direct correlation. The larger the bowl or pond, the larger the goldfish can grow. Similarly, the smaller the market in business, the lesser the growth potential.

2. NUMBER OF OTHER GOLDFISH IN THE BOWL OR POND = COMPETITION

GROWTH FACTOR: The number of goldfish in the same bowl or pond.

IMPACT: Inverse correlation. The more goldfish, the less growth. Similarly, the less competition in business, the more growth opportunity exists.

3. THE QUALITY OF THE WATER = THE ECONOMY

GROWTH FACTOR: The clarity and amount of nutrients in the water.

IMPACT: Direct correlation. The better the quality, the larger the growth. Similarly, the weaker the economy or capital markets in business, the more difficult it is too grow.

> **FACT**
>
> A malnourished goldfish in a crowded, cloudy environment may only grow to two inches (five centimeters).

4. THE FIRST 120 DAYS OF LIFE = STARTUP PHASE OR A NEW PRODUCT LAUNCH

GROWTH FACTOR: The nourishment and treatment received as a fry (baby goldfish).

IMPACT: Direct correlation. The lower the quality of the food, water, and treatment, the more the goldfish will be stunted for future growth. Similarly, in business, the stronger the leadership and capital for a start-up, the better the growth.

5. GENETIC MAKEUP = DIFFERENTIATION

GROWTH FACTOR: The genetic makeup of the goldfish.

IMPACT: Direct correlation. The poorer the genes or the less differentiated, the less the goldfish can grow. Similarly, in business, the more differentiated the product or service from the competition, the better the chance for growth.

> **FACT**
>
> The current *Guinness Book of World Records* holder for the largest goldfish hails from The Netherlands at a whopping 19 inches (50 centimeters). To put that in perspective, that's about the size of the average domestic cat.

WHICH OF THE FIVE FACTORS CAN YOU CONTROL?

Let's assume you have an existing product or service and have been in business for more than four months. Do you have any control over the market, your competition, or the economy? NO, NO, and NO.

The only thing you have control over is your business's genetic makeup or how you differentiate your product or service. In goldfish terms, how do you stand out in a sea of sameness?

Now, why the color pink?

CHAPTER 4

WHY PINK?

Pink is the sixth color in the Goldfish series. So why did we choose pink? There are a few reasons. First, pink is a color currently associated with women and girls. Second, pink is associated with differentiation and uniqueness. But it hasn't always been this way.

ORIGIN OF THE WORD

Pink was first used as a color name in the late 1600s. The golden age for pink was during was the Rococo Period in the 1700s. Pastel colors became fashionable in all the courts of Europe. Pink was particularly championed by the mistress of Louis XV, Madame de Pompadour.

Throughout the 1800s and into the early 1900s, pink ribbons or decorations were often worn by young boys in England. Boys were considered small men, and while men in England wore red uniforms, boys wore pink. Pink was seen as a more masculine color than blue. For example, a 1918 article in Earnshaw's Infants' Department explained that "the generally accepted rule is pink for the boys and blue for the girls. The reason is that pink, being a more decided and stronger color, is more suitable for the boy, while blue, which is more delicate and dainty, is prettier for the girl." This is the exact opposite of the way we now think about pink.

It wasn't until the mid-1900s that people started choosing pink for girls and blue for boys. This became the accepted norm in the 1940s. The tipping point for pink occurred in 1953 when the new First Lady of the United States, Mamie Eisenhower, wore a pink gown for the presidential inauguration of her husband, Dwight D. Eisenhower.

BREAST CANCER AWARENESS

In 1985, October was designated by the American Cancer Society as National Breast Cancer Awareness Month. The Susan G. Komen Foundation distributed pink ribbons to breast cancer survivors in 1991. The Breast Cancer Research Foundation chose a pink ribbon as their symbol in 1993. Since then, the month of October and the color pink have become synonymous with the cause of breast cancer research and treatment. For example, during October, male and female athletes wear pink to raise awareness for the cause.

Let's focus on this example for a moment because it illustrates both of our reasons for using pink. It's remarkable when National Football League players wear pink. When big, tough guys wear pink, people notice. This is because we now think of pink as a feminine color and therefore, it's unusual to see men wearing pink, especially when they are wearing helmets and trying to physically destroy each other.

This is also true in other sports. Pink has "reached a critical mass in unexpected places." When many younger players at the 2017 Men's U.S. Open Golf Tournament wore pink pants and pink shirts, it was so surprising that it prompted a *New York Times* fashion article. Vanessa Friedman wrote that "the amount of pink on view on Saturday was impossible to ignore.... This was pink-by-choice, pink as a core element of a competitive wardrobe." She argued that pink has become "a state of mind, or an idea, as opposed to a specific Pantone shade." It is now a "symbol of this particular moment in time, from the looser definitions of gender and gender stereotypes, to the refusal to be boxed in to a traditional set of dress code mores and expectations."

This is important. Colors don't have a gender. There is nothing inherently feminine or masculine in any particular shade. However, society has ascribed gender to certain colors, and when people challenge these arbitrary categories, it is different. It is unusual. It stands out.

DAVID RENDALL'S FREAK FACTOR

Another reason behind pink is the co-author of this book. David Rendall is the ultimate advocate for embracing weirdness and exploiting imperfection. David wears head to toe pink on stage. This includes, pink pants, pink shoes, pink socks, pink belt, and a pink watch. His shirts display his trademark pink Tyrannosaurus Rex. He even has a custom-made three-piece pink pinstripe suit, which he wears with a pink shirt, pink tie, and pink Chuck Taylor shoes.

When asked about all the pink, he says that his family was the inspiration. David and his wife, Stephanie, have three daughters, Sophia, Emma, and Anna. Even his dog is a female. During his speeches, he tells a series of funny stories about how living in a house full of women is gradually turning him into a woman. From pushing him to use exfoliating body wash to painting his toenails to telling him to trim his eyebrows, they are on a mission to make him more like them. Instead of pushing back, he has chosen to embrace his feminine side and the color that represents it—pink.

His unconventional commitment to pink makes him memorable to his audiences. David leaned in and pink has become inextricably linked to his brand. It's on the cover of his book. It's on his website. It's everywhere, even off-stage. Because he competes in Ironman triathlons and ultramarathons, he had his bike custom-painted pink. He also has a pink helmet, sunglasses, hat, tri-suit, and socks. Even his wedding ring is pink, thanks to Qalo.

Pink is a main differentiator for him. It makes him remarkable. David powers his business on referrals. He gets audience members to say, "You've got to hear this guy. He's funny and he wears pink pants and he talks about dyslexic billionaires and freakish arm wrestlers from Germany." More than once he's been approached in an airport by someone who recognized him because of his pink clothes. He receives pink gifts from his clients and fans, most notably, pink underwear and a pink cowboy hat. His Facebook feed is a constant barrage of interesting pink objects, like cars and buildings, sent from people all over the world.

But it didn't start this way. David didn't always wear pink. He didn't always want to stick out. He didn't want to be weird. He wanted to be normal and professional. He wanted to be accepted. He wanted to fit in. He wore normal pants, normal shirts, normal shoes, and normal ties. He wanted to meet other people's conception of what a successful person wore. He wanted people to take him seriously.

It's hard sometimes to go against the grain of what everybody else does because we wonder if people are going to like it. That is why we wrote this book. We want to show you the power of pink, the power of being different, the power of defying expectation, and the power of being weird.

This is something David learned in a very personal way and explained in his book, *The Freak Factor.*

> I spent my whole life getting in trouble because I couldn't sit still, be quiet, and do what I was told. Then at some point, as an adult, I realized I was getting paid to stand up and talk and run my own business. The very thing that people spent their whole life telling me not to do (my own parents used to call me "motor mouth") was the thing I was getting paid for. It was the thing that I was doing really well.
>
> I discovered that my weaknesses were strengths. I started to wonder whether that may be true for other

people and in business. I developed the concept of the Freak Factor, developed an assessment, wrote a book, and started gathering stories about how seemingly obvious weaknesses are also strengths and how the things that sometimes we're fixing to get better are actually the things we should be flaunting or amplifying or embracing.

It wouldn't be fair or consistent to tell other people to be freaks and to pursue an extraordinary path to success while behaving and dressing in a completely conventional way. This is another reason David started wearing pink. He had to practice what he preached. He had to walk the talk. He wanted to experiment, in his life and business, with the value of being strange. His experience has convinced him that there is tremendous value in living an uncommon life.

PINK-TRASH

David isn't the only one who's found an advantage in being pink. Kelly Buffalino started Pink-Trash in Wilmington, North Carolina, because she was unhappy with the poor service and high fees of other providers. She created a company focused on better service, environmental values, and low flat rates.

She chose pink because it's "her favorite color and the high visibility attracts new customers." As a breast cancer survivor, Kelly is also committed to supporting cancer treatment for local men and women. Her company does this through donations of time, money, and resources.

PINK SNOW PLOWS

While working on finalizing this book, David was a speaker at the Michigan Green Industry Association's annual trade show. As he walked to the ballroom, he felt a little conspicuous in his pink pants and pink shoes. All of the attendees were in the landscaping and snow removal business. As far as their dress, it was a sea of blue, green, black, and gray. There weren't a lot of bright colors, especially in the middle of winter. He wasn't sure this was an audience that would appreciate his pink wardrobe.

As he was standing in the back of the room,. waiting to go on stage, he bumped into the founder of Troy Clogg Landscape Associates. Troy said he loved the pink and explained that his employees wear pink uniforms and drive pink snow plows and pink trucks. They also sell pink road salt. Hot Pink Deicer is another company they founded and profits from each sale allow them to donate thousands of dollars each year to breast cancer patients who are struggling financially.

Talk about standing out. Have you ever seen a pink snow plow? Troy has learned that it pays to do things differently than everyone else in his industry, and pink is a key part of his differentiation strategy. It's also part of his mission to help cancer patients and their families.

T-MOBILE

T-Mobile is so committed to pink that they've trademarked their particular version of the color (RAL 4010). They call it magenta, and they aren't messing around. When Aio Wireless started using a similar color (Pantone 676C) in 2014, T-Mobile sued. They argued that "letting Aio continue to use a variant of magenta would cause [T-Mobile] irreparable harm." T-Mobile won the exclusive right to their shade of pink and apparently "nearby colors" as well.

Their CEO, John Legere, can nearly always be found wearing a pink t-shirt. That's unusual. Most big company CEOs wear suits, not t-shirts. Legere argues that pink and his casual style are part of the company's identity as the "uncarrier." It brands them as unique from all the other mobile giants who have chosen traditional CEOs and traditional colors, such as blue (AT&T), red (Verizon), yellow (Sprint), and blue/red (U.S. Cellular).

NURSE NEXT DOOR

In 2016, David had the opportunity to speak at Nurse Next Door's annual conference in Vancouver. The theme was Bold Pink. The company provides senior home health services. They set themselves apart by their use of distinctive bright pink cars that go from home to home. They developed a technique called *parketing*, a portmanteau for parking and marketing. Unwilling to buy billboards as a scrappy startup, Nurse Next Door would instead park their pink branded vehicles in high traffic areas to generate awareness. This unique approach attracted new owners, employees, and clients. Their CEO, Cathy Thorpe, believes that pink is representative of their disruptive approach to the industry.

Now that we've explored the meaning behind pink and goldfish, the next part of the book will focus on the seven different ways to bring your particular pink goldfish to life.

Ready to be F.L.A.W.S.O.M? Let's go...

THE TYPES
(THE WHAT)

CHAPTER 5

BECOMING F.L.A.W.S.O.M.

"Most of us spend our lives trying to be, and seem, 'perfect.'
We try to protect ourselves. It can sometimes be difficult
to drop the pretense and own up to your flaws and faults
– it takes courage. But what's the greatest risk?
Letting go of what other people think, or letting go of
how you feel, what you believe, and who you are?"

- Brené Brown[1], The Gifts of Imperfection

---

1. https://www.cosmopolitan.com.au/lifestyle/youre-flawesome-13814

31

In the 15th century the Japanese Shogun Ashikaga Yoshimasa sent for his favorite tea bowl. The broken bowl was in the process of being repaired. When it came back, it was fixed using ugly metal staples and other crude materials. It spurred him to ask his own craftsman to find a more aesthetically pleasing method of repair. The craftsmen used lacquer and gold to meticulously repair the cracks.

Photo Credit: Wikimedia Commons[2]

The shogun was extremely pleased with the result. Born out of the efforts of these craftsmen came the art of Kintsugi[3]. It is the practice of repairing broken pottery with lacquer dusted or mixed with powdered gold, silver, or platinum. Kintsugi in Japanese translates to "golden joinery." It has become a metaphor for embracing your breaks and flaws. It espouses the idea that the broken is more beau-

2. https://commons.wikimedia.org/wiki/File:Kintugi.jpg
3. https://en.wikipedia.org/wiki/Kintsugi

tiful than the pristine. The gold is used to intentionally call attention to the breaks instead of concealing them.

Collectors became so enamored with the new art that some were accused of deliberately smashing valuable pottery so it could be repaired with the golden seams of kintsugi. Here is the important takeaway from the art form of kintsugi. Mending the cracks makes the object more beautiful, not despite the flaws, but because of attention placed on them. This is the crux of the reasoning behind the pink goldfish concept—embracing what makes you weird or weak. In the words of author and speaker Tammy Lenski[4], we should be "revering, perhaps even illuminating, the flaws that make us unique—one of a kind and imperfectly special."

PORTMANTEAU

A portmanteau is a French word for a small suitcase. It also describes when parts of multiple words are combined to make a new word. For example, by blending smoke and fog to create smog. Or vlog, from video, web, and log. A portmanteau relates to a singular concept that the combined word describes. A portmanteau differs from a compound word, which does not involve the truncation of parts of the stems of the blended words.

Our personal favorite portmanteau for a brand is Velcro. It is a combination of two French words. The "vel" is from velour (fabric) and the "cro" is from crochet (hook). In 2017, the Velcro company made a video of its lawyers imploring the public[5] not to call a hook and loop fastener by its trademarked name of Velcro.

---

4.   https://lenski.com/relationship-conflict-resolution-kintsugi/

5.   https://www.velcro.com/about-us/dontsayvelcro/

The video by the agency Walk West has generated millions of views. Once a brand name becomes generic, the brand name is in jeopardy of losing its trademark registration.

Photo Credit: YouTube

The portmanteau we use for *Pink Goldfish* is FLAWSOM. It is a combination of FLAWS and AWESOME—the simple idea that your flaws hold the key to what makes you awesome. The concept of flawsome isn't new. The term was originated by both Trendspotting and the supermodel Tyra Banks. Put those two together and you have the portmanteau of Trendbank or Spottyr. Let's look at both sources:

> According to Trendspotting in 2012[6], consumers don't expect brands to be flawless. In fact, consumers will embrace brands that are FLAWSOME: brands that are still brilliant despite having flaws; even being flawed (and being open about it) can be awesome.

> According to Tyra Banks, FLAWSOME is used to describe something that is awesome because of its flaws. She advocates for us to embrace the flaws in our bod-

ies and own them for they are simply flawsome. Tyra launched the Flawsome Ball to benefit her TZONE Foundation in 2012[7].

More Than a Portmanteau

In addition to the flawsom portmanteau, we've chosen to make an acronym out of it. Each letter in the F.L.A.W.S.O.M. framework represents one of seven types of Pink Goldfish:

F is for Flaunting

L is for Lopsiding

A is for Antagonizing

W is for Withholding

S is for Swerving

O is for Opposing

M is for Micro-weirding

Next, let's explore each. Flaunting is first...

---

7. https://www.rachaelrayshow.com/celebs/8265_Tyra_Banks_Flawsome_Ball_Celebration_of_the_Muffin_Top/

CHAPTER 6

FLAUNTING

"If you can't fix it, feature it."

– Gerald Weinberg

THE "F" IN F.L.A.W.S.O.M. STANDS FOR FLAUNTING

According to the Encarta Dictionary[8], flaunt means "to parade without shame. Show something off—to display something ostentatiously." Our interpretation of the word is that flaunting is positive. Flaunting is about being unapologetic about your organization's flaws. You take pride in your organization's unique characteristics. You emphasize them, accentuate them, feature them, highlight them, expose them, call attention to them, and openly display them. You definitely aren't trying to hide them or fix them.

Too often, we are uncomfortable with what makes us weird. Our goal in this book isn't simply to help you become comfortable with what makes you weak or weird in business. We want you to parade those weaknesses without shame. To show them off.

This might sound unwise, because this isn't the way most organizations operate. It isn't what most business books recommend. Managers have been taught to find and fix weakness, to seek perfection.

FINDING STRENGTH IN WEAKNESS

Established in 1919, W.K. Buckley formulated a cough syrup called Buckley's Mixture. Noted for its strongly unpleasant taste, its ingredients include ammonium carbonate, potassium bicarbonate, camphor, menthol, Canada balsam, pine needle oil, and a tincture of capsicum. Translation: the mixture tastes horrible and is not for the faint of heart.

---

8. https://books.google.com/books?id=ICylixhKK4QC&pg=PA544&lpg=PA544&dq=Encarta+Dictionary+flaunt+means+%E2%80%9Cto+parade+without+shame.+Show+something+off+%E2%80%93+to+display+something+ostentatiously.&source=bl&ots=jHZRazyb6c&sig=ETmrbR6MCCQD1uUJJPmXTJWitSc&hl=en&sa=X&ved=0ahUKEwiv157Rr-nYAhUQG6wKHYitD38Q6AEIJzAA

After W.K.'s death in 1978, Buckley's adopted son, Frank, became the president of the company. In the mid-1980s, Frank became the spokesperson for the brand. He commissioned research and found that Buckley's was notorious for two reasons. Consumers consistently spoke to its efficacy and its lousy taste. Frank decided to flaunt the taste and began promoting a new slogan for the brand, "It tastes awful. And it works."

People swear by it. And at it.

It tastes awful. And it works.

Their cough syrup is nasty, and they are proud of that. Buckley's didn't try to hide it or mask the flavor like the competition. Instead, they made the bad taste their focus. In advertisements, Frank compared the taste to trash bag leakage and sweaty gym socks. The implicit message is that it works because it tastes awful.

The "bad taste" campaign increased Buckley's market share[9] by over 550 percent in the Canadian cough & cold category. The campaign won numerous advertising awards and was subsequently launched in the Caribbean, Australia, New Zealand, and the U.S.

In 2002, the brand was acquired by Novartis. Kironmoy Datta[10], senior brand manager for Novartis Consumer Health, says that "Buckley's isn't for everyone.... We made a conscious choice to not

9. http://www.buckleys.ca/about/history
10. http://onwardmag.com/how-flaunting-your-weaknesses-can-build-trust/

be everything to everyone." It takes courage to call attention to existing weaknesses, but it takes even more courage to make those weaknesses appear worse, to exaggerate and flaunt them.

Sometimes a pink goldfish tastes unapologetically awful.

Buckley's Footnote: Back in 2013, Buckley's was not available for sale in the U.S. due to factory issues. At the time, it had been reputed to sell on eBay for 10 times the original price.

Flaunting is the cornerstone of the F.L.A.W.S.O.M. framework. We've created the flaunting matrix to delineate how much and what you flaunt. The Y axis in the matrix stands for the amount of weirdness or normalcy:

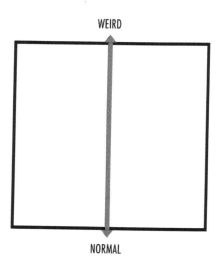

Weird is what makes you different or unique in business. What is weird is usually seen as a weakness or a flaw because it doesn't conform to the established model of success. Doing something abnormal is often seen as doing it the "wrong way."

Normal represents the standards within your industry. Normal defines the "right way." Normal is usually synonymous with strong. If everyone is doing it, then it must be a good thing. The X axis represents doing "more" or doing "less" of what makes you either weird or normal:

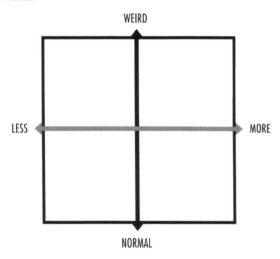

UNDERSTANDING THE QUADRANTS

The flaunting matrix contains four quadrants:

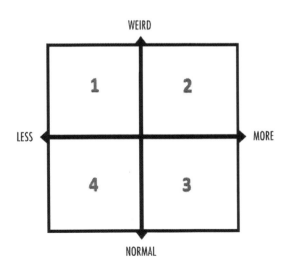

Each quadrant in the flaunting matrix is represented by an animal. The first quadrant, the top left, represents doing less of what makes you weird. It is the **COW** quadrant:

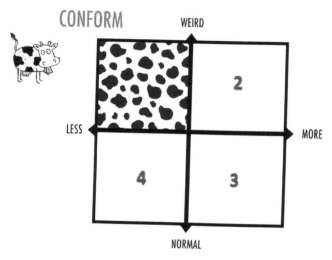

Why a Cow? Every cow is unique. Their spots are like finger-prints. No two cows are alike. Yet, cows are blissfully unaware of their uniqueness. Establish a cowpath and cows will never stray from it. This is the CONFORM quadrant.

The second quadrant, the top right, represents doing more of what makes you weird. It is the **PEACOCK** quadrant:

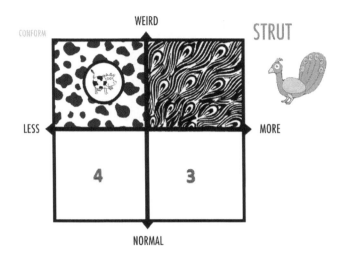

Why a Peacock? Like cows and their spots, the feathers on a peacock are unique. Unlike cows, they own it. Their uniqueness is a signature part of who they are. They purposefully preen and flaunt their feathers to stand out among the flock. This is the STRUT quadrant.

The third quadrant, the bottom right, represents doing more of what makes you normal. It is the **ZEBRA** quadrant:

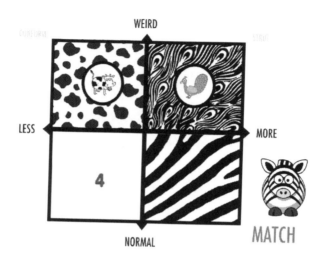

Why a Zebra? Zebras are black with white stripes. Their striping is determined by genetics. Even though zebras are unique, their individual stripes are indistinguishable among other zebras. Their stripes create a blending effect, making it impossible for an individual zebra to stand out among the herd. This is good for safety as predators see the herd as one huge object, but it makes standing out a non-starter. You can't add stripes and be different here. It's just more of the same. This is the MATCH quadrant.

The fourth quadrant, the bottom left, represents doing less of what makes you normal. It is the **POLAR BEAR** quadrant:

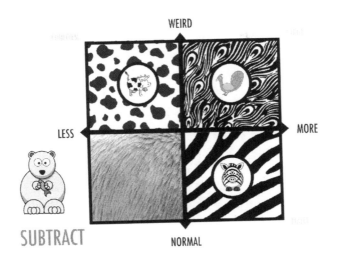

Why a Polar Bear? Polar bears aren't white. Their fur is translucent because their individual hair is hollow. The fur absorbs the light and takes away all of the colors in the spectrum so they appear white. Generally, polar bears avoid the herd and live solitary lives. This is the SUBTRACT quadrant.

THE FLAUNTING ZONE

We will advocate for staying within the "flaunting zone" to differentiate yourself in business:

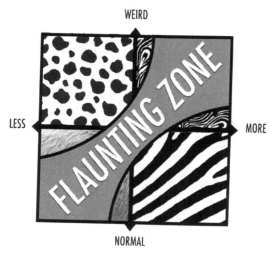

The goal is to flaunt that you do LESS of what makes you NORMAL *or* flaunt that you do MORE of what makes you WEIRD.

FLAUNTING YOUR WEIRDNESS AND WEAKNESS

Let's look at four more companies that embrace the concept of Flaunting.

1. **Alt Hotels does less** – Alt Hotels is a Canadian chain "offering a unique alternative to conventional hotels." Instead of just withholding the services that most customers expect, they created a campaign that flaunts all the things you won't find at their hotels. It's called "we do less."

Each of the five ads focuses on what they don't do and what they do instead. They are attracting the customers who want what they have and repelling the customers who want what they don't have.

We **don't** have a mini bar.   We **do** have a hip lounge.

We **don't** have a concierge.   We **do** have an app with all the hot spots.

We **don't** have a pool.   We **do** have a pool table.

We **don't** offer room service.   We **do** have fresh grab-and-go meals.

We **don't** have a bellman.   We **do** have a versatile helpful staff.

Alt Hotels doesn't apologize for their flaws. Each weakness is deliberately designed. They don't exceed expectations. They don't even meet expectations. They do less.

Sometimes a pink goldfish is a hotel that does less.

2. **Planet Fitness hates fit people** – The Grondahl brothers started Planet Fitness in New Hampshire in 1992. Their differentiation strategy is to provide low-cost memberships and an accepting environment for people who are joining a gym for the first time or who only work out sporadically.

Their advertising promotes Planet Fitness as a "no judgement zone," but that isn't really true. They won't judge you for being out of shape. They won't judge you for skipping workouts. They won't judge you for how you look or what you wear. But they will judge you if you're really fit, if you're really intense, or if you try really hard. If you grunt or breathe hard or slam the weights, they'll ask you to leave and not come back.

Planet Fitness is accepting if you have a dad bod or a muffin top, but they are antagonistic if you are a bodybuilder or musclehead. They deliberately and publicly exclude customers with those goals and habits. Their advertising campaigns openly ridicule people who are passionate about being strong and fit. Those ads simultaneously attract the customers Planet Fitness wants to serve while repelling the customers they want to exclude.

Flaunt means to parade without shame. Planet Fitness isn't ashamed of how they openly discriminate against hyper-fit people in order to help their members workout without intimidation or fear of being shamed.

Sometimes a pink goldfish is a gym for people who don't go to the gym.

3. **RyanAir embraces unpopularity** – RyanAir flew for the first time in Ireland in 1984. Since then they have grown into Europe's biggest carrier. The company has always prided itself on cheap no-frills flights. However, it fundamentally fails to deliver a positive flying experience for consumers, and its customer service is famed for its bad attitude.

RyanAir routinely tops the consumer surveys for the least popular airline, an honor it received again in 2017. CEO Michael O'Leary is renowned for his controversial comments, such as, "We don't want to hear your sob stories." or "What part of 'no refund' don't you understand?" According to *Forbes*[11], likeability isn't integral to his leadership style.

Does RyanAir make excuses for the poor level of service? Absolutely not. They flaunt it. In 2013, the brand launched its very own "*I Hate Ryanair*" website.

Here are just a few of the things customers complain about:

---

11. https://www.forbes.com/sites/forbescoachescouncil/2017/07/19/why-we-only-need-one-degree-shifts-in-life-and-business/2/

- a 70 euro charge to print a boarding pass at the airport

- reducing the number of airplane bathrooms

- no seat back pockets

- no water served on flights

- a six euro charge to pay with a credit card

- no air sickness bags

- inconvenient airport locations

- a clunky website

Instead of trying to resolve these complaints, RyanAir uses their negative reputation to threaten further reductions in service. These empty threats generate additional free publicity. Here are a few examples of changes they announced, but had no intention of actually implementing:

- charging one euro to use the toilet

- creating a standing-room only section

- charging overweight passengers a fat tax

- requiring passengers to carry checked luggage to the plane

Even though they pledged to change their ways in 2014, they still ended 2017 as the lowest-rated airline in Europe. This was due to their handling of massive flight cancellations during the holiday season. They've also been ranked as the worst service of any company in Europe, not just the worst airline. In January 2018, they announced new size restrictions and charges for carry-on bags. Only one (very) small bag is allowed for free. Any additional bags will cost at least five euros.

O'Leary was recently asked if he was concerned about the company's negative image. He responded with this provocative statement. "Our booking engine is full of passengers who have sworn they will never fly with us again." Flying RyanAir will save you money, but it will be painful. They know it and they flaunt it.

Sometimes a pink goldfish is an airline everyone hates.

4. **Mini embraces small** – Americans love big vehicles. Big trucks and SUVs are the preferred means of transportation for millions of U.S. drivers. That fact made BMW's introduction of the Mini to the United States very interesting.

What would they do? Would they downplay the car's small size? At the time, it was about two feet shorter than the average compact car. Would they ignore size and focus on other features? Nope. They flaunted its tiny proportions. They exaggerated how little it was by comparing it to mobile phones and by putting a Mini in the bed of a pickup truck.

As YoungMe Moon explains in *Different - Escaping the Competitive Herd*, "It took its biggest possible wart and made it even bigger. All of its advertising seems to say 'it's even smaller than you think.'" This was intentional.

Alex Bogusky and his ad agency, Crispin Porter + Bogusky (CP+B), have been the creators of many well-known advertising campaigns. Among those was the introduction of the Mini to America. Its success was based on flaunting the weaknesses of Mini, not minimizing them. Instead of hiding qualities that seemed negative—such as its tiny proportions—CP+B exploited them.

According to Bogusky, "It's part of your job as a marketer to find the truths in a company, and you let them shine through in whatever weird way it might be. Naturally, that risks pissing someone off." Mini is small. It's obvious from the name. So, they flaunt it.

Sometimes a pink goldfish is tiny car that fits in the trunk of your other car.

The F in F.L.A.W.S.O.M. is Flaunting, parading without shame. Let's move on to the L...

CHAPTER 7

LOPSIDING

*"True differentiation is rarely a function of well-roundedness;
it is typically a function of lopsidedness."*

- Youngme Moon, Different - Escaping the Competitive Herd

THE "L" IN F.L.A.W.S.O.M. STANDS FOR LOPSIDING

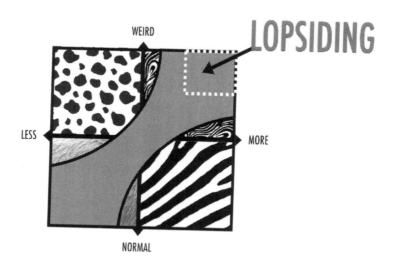

Most brands are trying to be balanced and well-rounded. It's interesting to note that synonyms for balanced include: sane, right, normal, and stable. Those sound like worthy goals. Be the perfect amount of everything. Be the best of all worlds. Make everyone happy. Eliminate flaws, minimize them, decrease them, diminish them, and lessen them. We think this is the wrong approach.

Lopsiding is about being unbalanced, imperfect, unstable, and odd. Let's stop here for a second. Antonyms for unbalanced (lopsided) include: crazy, insane, and unsound. Those don't sound like promising descriptions of brand strategy but bear with us. Lopsiding involves amplifying, not reducing, your brand's flaws. We want you to expand them, magnify them, increase them, turn them up, exaggerate them, and then supersize them.

Lopsiding is on one of the two extreme ends of the flaunting zone. Brands here are purposefully doing MORE of what makes them weird or weak. This is flaunting weaknesses at its best. You aren't just proud of your weaknesses, you are expanding and extending them. You are doubling down to accentuate your flaws.

Lopsiding is not for the faint of heart. It takes courage to call attention to existing weaknesses. It takes even more courage to make those weaknesses worse, to exaggerate them. That's what Hardee's did, and it saved their company.

Here is a letter from Andy Puzder, former CEO of CKE Restaurants (parent of Carl's Jr. and Hardee's), on the back of a bag for a Philly Cheesesteak Thickburger:

> When I became president of Hardee's Restaurants, we were selling so many things that we had truly become a 'jack of all trades and master of none.' Unfortunately, in today's competitive fast food world, that wasn't cutting it. The chain needed to become known for doing something really well again. So I challenged my menu development folks to come up with a new line of burgers that would make people say 'Wow! I can't believe I can get burgers that good at a fast-food place.' And they did. They came up with Thickburgers.

It is important to note that Carl's Jr. and Hardee's were closing many of their stores before developing this new line of burgers. Even more importantly, most other fast food companies were furiously adding healthy options to their menu. In response to criticism about the negative health effects of their offerings, fast food outlets were offering water, fruit, and salads. Hardee's moved in the opposite direction[12]. In essence, they were saying, "our food is fat and nasty and will make you fat and nasty." And it worked.

They succeeded by amplifying the weaknesses of fast food while everyone else was busy trying to moderate those same weaknesses. They took fast food, which was already tremendously unhealthy, and they lopsided it to make it even unhealthier. They took fatty foods and made them fattier. They took nasty food and made it nastier. And it worked.

Our personal favorite menu item from Hardee's is the Aporkalypse. It combines ham + sausage + bacon on a biscuit or a burrito.

Sometimes a pink goldfish is wrapped in bacon and covered in sausage.

Here are four more examples of brands that are intentionally lopsided:

1. **Phil Hansen and his shake** – While in art school, Phil Hansen developed an uncontrollable shake in his hand due to his pointillism work. In his words, "It was actually good for some things, like mixing a can of paint or shaking a Polaroid, but at the time this was really doomsday. This was the destruction of my dream of becoming an artist." Hansen dropped out.

---

12. http://onwardmag.com/how-flaunting-your-weaknesses-can-build-trust/

But after a few years, he just couldn't stay away from art. A trip to a neurologist revealed permanent nerve damage in his hand. His doctor looked at his squiggly lines and challenged Phil, "Well, why don't you just embrace the shake?"

He went home and let his hand shake when drawing. The result was scribble pictures. It felt great for Hansen. He realized he just had to find a different approach to making the art that he wanted. Hansen began experimenting by:

- dipping his feet in paint and walking on a canvas.

- building a 3D structure consisting of two-by-fours and creating a 2D image by burning it on the two-by-fours with a blowtorch.

Hansen began to understand that limitations could actually drive creativity. He pushed himself further and began to lopside his creativity. Some of his creations have included:

- using hundreds of real, live worms to make an image.

- using a pushpin to tattoo a banana.

- painting a picture with hamburger grease.

Limitations may be the most unlikely of places to harness creativity but perhaps one of the best ways to get ourselves out of ruts, rethink categories, and challenge accepted norms. And instead of telling each other to seize the day, maybe we can remind ourselves every day to seize the limitation.

Want to learn more about Phil Hansen and his journey? Check out his 10-minute TED talk[13]. It has been viewed over two million times.

---

13. https://www.ted.com/talks/phil_hansen_embrace_the_shake/transcript

Sometimes a pink goldfish is embracing constraints and doubling down on them.

2. CrossFit wants to hurt you – CrossFit was founded by Greg Glassman and Lauren Jenai in 2000. It is promoted as more than just a method for working out. It is also a sport, a philosophy, and, for some, a religion. The goal of CrossFit is partially explained in its name. The workouts are designed to make participants fit in every major area such as muscular strength, cardiovascular capacity, and flexibility.

A CrossFit gym is called a "box" and there are more than 13,000 boxes around the world. Most of the boxes are intentionally rugged. They are very hot or very cold, depending on the weather. They are loud, dirty, and smelly. There are no shiny machines. Most aren't neatly organized.

While completing the WODs (workout of the day), people are sweating profusely, grunting, screaming, yelling, and sometimes crying. They are pushing their bodies to the brink. No one is wiping down machines or even their own bodies. It's a free-for-all. Cross-Fit members are also famous for being fanatical evangelists for this unique approach to exercise and life. If someone does CrossFit, they will talk about it in almost every conversation. They brag that their warm-up is harder than most other people's entire workout.

High intensity interval training is a hallmark of CrossFit WODs. These workouts vary dramatically with the goal of muscle con-fusion. Instead of consistent, routine, and programmed exercise, CrossFit attempts to stimulate fitness gains by challenging the body in surprising and unpredictable ways. CrossFit isn't for everyone. It isn't even for most healthy people who exercise regularly. It cer-tainly isn't for people with a casual approach to exercise.

CrossFit's massive success led to the creation of the CrossFit Games, which are sponsored by Reebok. The winners of the event are crowned as the "fittest man on earth" and the "fittest woman on earth." Thousands of people compete around the world for a chance to participate in the games. Thousands more attend the multi-day event as spectators. Netflix has produced multiple documentaries of the games called "Fittest on Earth."

CrossFit is lopsided. It is intentionally difficult. It is purposefully extreme. It is about being bigger, better, faster, and stronger. That is what makes it so attractive and so energizing for some people. CrossFit doesn't need to make their WODs easier. They don't need to tone it down, ease up, or lower their standards. They go farther and appeal to people who want to go farther.

By the way, CrossFit enthusiasts refer to Planet Fitness as "Planet Fitless."

Sometimes a pink goldfish is hot and long and hard.

3. **McDonald's can't make you healthy** – This chapter started with the story of the outrageous offerings at Hardee's and Carl's Jr. They were able to differentiate by creating unhealthy options for customers at the same time that other fast food chains like McDonald's were creating healthy options.

Now it looks like McDonald's is changing course. They aren't necessarily creating new high-calorie, high-fat items, they're just removing many of the more wholesome ones. According to the *Wall Street Journal*[14] in March 2017, "McDonald's has decided to shift focus back to core products. After losing about 500 million U.S. orders over the past five years over failed attempts to widen its customer base, the fast-food chain said it is going to embrace its iden-

---

14. https://www.wsj.com/articles/mcdonalds-to-expand-mobile-delivery-as-it-plots-future-1488390702

tity as an affordable fast-food chain and stop chasing after people who will rarely eat there."

A customer survey showed that they were losing customers to other fast food restaurants, not to outlets offering healthy foods. They also saw that their own healthy options weren't selling very well. In response, McDonald's is removing some of their low-calorie, low-fat menu items like oatmeal, wraps, and salads. Apparently, their customers are lopsided, and they need to be lopsided too.

Sometimes a pink goldfish is giving people what they want.

4. **Velveeta strikes gold** – The last Lopsiding example comes from the *Golden Goldfish* book in this series. Gold is based on the simple premise that all customers are not created equal. It advocates that paying attention to your top customers is a recipe for success. Joseph Juran, who coined the Pareto Principle, espoused the importance of taking care of your "vital few." He found that for the vast majority of businesses, 80 percent of profitability is generated by just 20 percent of customers.

In the *Harvard Business Review* article[15] "Make Your Best Customers Even Better," authors Eddie Yoon, Steve Carlotti, and Dennis Moore bring this to life with the example of Kraft Velveeta cheese. In 2012, the Velveeta brand experienced its third consecutive year of declining sales. What could Kraft do to reverse this trend? Could they get new or lapsed customers to try the product? Could they get infrequent purchasers to buy the product more consistently?

The brand managers studied how the brand was being consumed. Research found the top 10 percent of Velveeta buyers account for over 50 percent of all sales of the product. And these consumers were not getting enough Velveeta in their lives. Kraft decided to focus on this key segment of 2.4 million consumers. The results

---

15. https://hbr.org/2014/03/make-your-best-customers-even-better

are anything but cheesy. New product spin-offs totaling over $100 million in additional sales have been game changing. It has shifted a paradigm for Kraft. According to marketing director Greg Gallagher:

> The previous thinking was that the quickest, easiest path to growth was to identify light users or lapsed users. But when we talked to superconsumers, we learned that in fact they wanted to use Velveeta more— they were starving for it.

All customers are not created equal. Lopsiding is doing more for your best ones. In the words of Yoon, Carlotti, and Moore, "Show the love to those that love you the most."

Sometimes a pink goldfish is also a golden goldfish and it's made of melted cheese.

The L in F.L.A.W.S.O.M. is for Lopsiding, accentuating your flaws. Let's move on to the A...

CHAPTER 8

ANTAGONIZING

"If you're not eliciting a negative response from someone, then you're probably not very compelling to anyone."

- Sally Hogshead, Fascinate

THE "A" IN F.L.A.W.S.O.M. STANDS FOR ANTAGONIZING

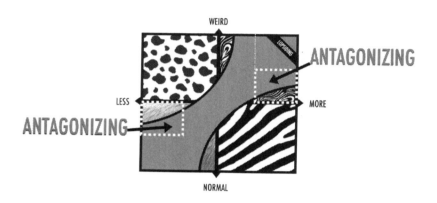

Antagonizing is about polarizing, alienating, repelling, and taunting. In some ways, it is a combination of everything we've covered so far. You do more of what some customers don't want (Lopsiding) and then you brag about it (Flaunting).

When most brands encounter irate customers, they try to soothe or placate or pacify or calm or reassure. They want to win over or win back the irate customer. They want to hug them and exceed their expectations. During planning sessions, they use focus groups and customer surveys. The goal is to discover what people want and then give it to them. That's not what we're recommending.

We want you to intentionally exasperate, irritate, provoke, aggravate, and instigate hostility. Go out of your way to rub people the wrong way. Try to earn a few more one-star reviews on Amazon or Yelp. Tell your employees to increase the number of complaints. Make customer satisfaction less of a priority. Ring a bell in the office every time you get a nasty email. Try it. We promise, the more some people hate you, the more other people will love you.

Antagonizing occupies two sides of the flaunting zone. It is both the act of doing MORE of what makes you weak or weird and doing LESS of what is considered normal and good by others. Here's a great example of Antagonizing:

The Alamo Drafthouse Cinema was founded by Tim and Karrie League in 1998 in Austin, Texas. They have 29 locations across the United States, more than half of which are in Texas. Their strictly enforced policy of movie-going etiquette has made them both famous and infamous. They have clear rules that everyone has to follow. If someone breaks the rules, they are punished.

Many brands increasingly monitor the internet for negative product reviews and contact reviewers to remedy complaints, persuading some to revise reviews with higher ratings. Not the Alamo Drafthouse Cinema; they take movie-going seriously. They are obsessed with the cinema experience, and they know their approach will make some people unhappy. And that it will make some very unhappy.

They maintain strict rules for both talking and/or texting during a movie, and for late arrivals. Additionally, children under two are not allowed in the theater except for special events. Unsupervised minors are not allowed either unless they are 15 years old and have been accepted into a membership program, which includes training on the theater's many policies. As you can see, they take this seriously. You have to take a class to be admitted into a movie theater.

Alamo knows that their approach isn't popular with everyone. Tim League posted this explanation on their website, "When we adopted our strict no talking policy back in 1997, we knew we were going to alienate some of our patrons. That was the plan. If you can't change your behavior and be quiet (or unilluminated) during a movie, then we don't want you at our venue."

Violators of the rules are given a warning and are then subject to removal. And they will remove you. One moviegoer found this out the hard way in 2011. And she did not take it well. It was so epic that Alamo turned it into a PSA that they show before the movie starts.

> **Alamo Drafthouse:** *At the Alamo Drafthouse, we have a simple rule: If you talk or text during a movie, we kick you out. Sometimes, that pisses the movie talker off. What follows is an actual voicemail a customer left us after being kicked out.*

> **Customer:** Yeah, I was wondering if you guys actually enjoy treating your customers like pieces of sh*t? Because that's how I felt when I went to the Alamo Drafthouse.

> Okay? You know what? I didn't know that I wasn't supposed to text in your little crappy ass theater. It was too f*cking dark in that place to even find my seat. All right? I was using my phone as a flashlight to get to my f*ckin' seat.

> So excuse me for using my phone in USA Magnited State of America, where you are free to text in a theater. I was not aware that I couldn't text in your theater. All right?

> I've texted in all the other theaters in Austin. And no one ever gave a f*ck about what me, I was doing with my f*ckin' phone. All right? And it was on silent. It wasn't on loud. It wasn't bothering anybody.

> You guys obviously were being assh*les to me. And I'm sure that's what you do. You know, to rip people

off. You take my money and you throw me out. You know?

I will never be comin' back to your Alamo Drafthouse or whatever. I'd rather go to a regularlier theater where people are actually polite. You know?

I'm gonna tell everyone about how sh*tty you are. And I'm pretty sure you guys are being assh*les on purpose. So thanks for making me feel like a customer. Thanks for takin' my money, assh*le!

Alamo Drafthouse: You're welcome! Thanks for not coming back to the Alamo, texter!

League is unapologetic. "We wanted to take a hard stand and say that those people are not welcome at the Alamo Drafthouse. So [we] will get rid of those people and just make it a better place for the rest of the movie-going public."

By the way, the "Don't Talk PSA | Angry Voicemail" also went viral outside of the theater. The video has garnered over 4.5 million views on YouTube and was featured by Anderson Cooper on CNN.

Alamo prides itself as a cinema built by movie fans for movie fans. They purposely embraced this complaint to emphasize how serious they are about movies. They've done more of what makes them weird as a business. If you don't like it, you can leave. If they don't like you, they'll make you leave. If you complain, they'll put you on the big screen.

Sometimes a pink goldfish is a list of strictly enforced rules.

Let's look at four more companies that antagonize customers:

1. **Dick's Last Resort trains obnoxious servers** – Dick's Last Resort is a casual restaurant chain with several locations across the United States. After failing in their effort to create a fine-dining restaurant, they developed a completely different approach. Instead of training their servers to be polite and helpful, they teach them to be rude and obnoxious. They want to provide customers with bad service. For example, napkins aren't placed on the table. If someone wants a napkin, one is thrown at them.

Their servers aren't the only thing that is rude at Dick's. They sell offensive t-shirts and bumper stickers proclaiming that "Real Women Love Dick's" and "I Love Dick's." Their tasteless menu includes the "Dolly Parton: a voluptuously grilled chicky breast."

Professor Herbert Sherman submitted this example to us. "I ate at this restaurant and this write up by Mike Michalowicz[16] is quite true."

> Instead of trying to fix weaknesses, smart leaders will turn the tables and make their weakness, or even an industry weakness, a competitive advantage. A wonderful example in the restaurant industry is Dick's Last Resort[17]. Like all restaurants who struggle with the occasional rude waiter, Dick's could have tried to fix this industry-wide weakness. Instead they turned the weakness into their greatest strength. Known to have the 'most obnoxious wait staff in the world,' Dick's built a whole system around exploiting an industry weakness. They hire and train people to be obnoxious (while the competition tries to fix it), and Dick's has grown explosively.

16. http://www.mikemichalowicz.com/turn-biggest-weakness-biggest-strength/
17. http://www.dickslastresort.com/

Other restaurants have succeeded with this antagonistic model. Ed Debevic's was founded in 1984 in Chicago. It's a 1950's themed diner with burgers, fries, shakes, and really rude servers. Similarly, Ben Baker told us about The Elbow Room Cafe in Vancouver that tells customers "food and service is our name, abuse is our game!" and offers menu items such as Big Ass Pancakes and "I Have No Imagination" omelettes.

Sometimes a pink goldfish is rude service.

2. **Progressive knows that people hate Flo** – Progressive is one of the largest insurance companies in the United States. The company was started in Ohio in 1937 by Jack Green and Joseph Lewis. One of their initial differentiation strategies was focusing on insurance for risky drivers. Then, in 2008, they added Flo.

Flo is the extremely enthusiastic and upbeat fictional customer service representative in the bright white uniform with the name tag. Some people love her. They think she is funny and cute and quirky and energetic and memorable. Others find her incredibly annoying. She's been compared to the Aflac duck with the grating voice of Gilbert Gottfried. Haters describe her as "irritating, creepy, dorky, unattractive, and weird."

Flo's commercials appear on lists of the most disliked advertisements[18], and there are I Hate Flo groups on Facebook, including one calling for No Mo Flo.

Flo is antagonizing. Flo is polarizing. Many people dislike her, but everyone knows who she is. And that's the point. She has helped Progressive get, and keep, the attention of potential customers.

3. **Five Guys Burgers and Fries doesn't care about your peanut allergy** -- If you need to fly and you have a peanut allergy, the

---

18. https://www.huffingtonpost.com/tom-alderman/go-with-the-flo---or-mayb_b_5085168.html

airline will try to protect you. They won't give out peanuts on your flight. They'll also make an announcement to request that people don't consume any peanut products on the plane.

If you want a burger and you have a peanut allergy, Five Guys won't do anything to protect you. They fry everything in peanut oil, there are piles of peanuts stacked everywhere and peanut shells all over the floor. If a person with a peanut allergy goes into Five Guys, they may be risking their life.

As you can imagine, this leads to a lot of questions and complaints. Here is how Five Guys responds on their website:

> If so many people are allergic to peanuts, why does Five Guys continue to offer them? Over the last 20 years, peanuts have become part of the Five Guys identity. We by no means want to exclude guests from our store, but at the same time we would not want to disappoint our peanut-eating guests. We make sure that we have signage on our doors and in our restaurants about the fact that we serve peanuts in bulk containers as we would never want someone to risk their health by coming into our restaurants.

I'm not sure if it's possible to be more antagonizing than this. It is one thing for a product or service to make potential customers unhappy. It is another thing for a product or service to physically harm or kill potential customers.

Five Guys isn't even selling the peanuts. They give them away. It costs them millions of dollars a year to provide peanuts for free to every customer, but they won't stop. They know that their peanuts threaten people's health, but they refuse to remove them because it such an important part of their brand identity.

Sometimes a pink goldfish causes an allergic reaction.

4. **Marmite tastes awful, and it's not for everyone** – Marmite is brewer's yeast, a byproduct of the beer-making process. It was originally produced in England by the Marmite Food Extract Company starting in 1902. It is currently made by Unilever. The product is concentrated into a thick brown paste that has a very strong flavor and an incredibly salty taste. It is usually spread thinly on bread or toast.

So is Marmite disgusting or delightful? Yes. It's both. Many consumers are devoted to it. Many others despise it.

To highlight Marmite's polarizing effect, the "love it or hate it" advertising campaign was created. It has been so successful that Marmite has become a metaphor in England for anything that evokes a strongly positive response from some and a strongly negative response from others. Marmite is kind of like Flo from Progressive, some people love it and other people hate it.

Marmite is shining a light on the offensively unique flavor of their product. They aren't trying to hide it or pretend it's delicious. They aren't trying to tone it down. They aren't creating a light version or a low salt version. In fact, they did the exact opposite. In 2010, they introduced an extra-strength version, Marmite XO. If you thought Marmite was bad, they made it even worse and the first shipments sold out as soon as they landed on store shelves. Marmite is embracing their fans and antagonizing their haters. Marmite isn't for everyone.

Sometimes a pink goldfish is a paste of thick extra-strength brown yeast.

The A in F.L.A.W.S.O.M. is for Antagonizing, being polarizing. Let's move on to the W...

CHAPTER 9

WITHHOLDING

*"The more constraints one imposes, the more one frees one's self.
And the arbitrariness of the constraint serves only to
obtain precision of execution."*

- Igor Stravinsky

THE W IN F.L.A.W.S.O.M. STANDS FOR WITHHOLDING

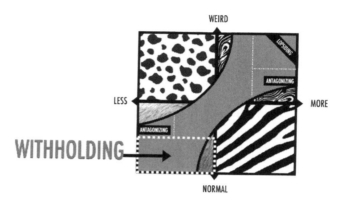

Most brands are trying to be strong, and they want to get stronger. They want to be powerful. This seems to make sense. Be the best. Do more. Expand. Grow. Offer more features, more products, more services, and more locations. But maybe there's a better way.

Withholding is about limitations, restrictions, boundaries, and constraints. That sounds obviously negative. Don't great brands offer freedom? Don't customers want services to be unlimited? Shouldn't the best organizations be everywhere all the time? Even if we don't serve everyone, we certainly want more customers, don't we?

Lopsiding is about doing more of what makes you weak and weird, not more of what everyone else is doing. This chapter is all about doing LESS, but not less of what makes you weak and weird. Instead, we want you to do less of what makes other brands normal and strong.

Withholding involves offering fewer options, fewer locations, fewer features, fewer products, fewer services, fewer hours, fewer perks, and fewer discounts. Avoiding is deliberately and relentlessly shrinking the things that everyone else is expanding.

Withholding sits at the opposite end of flaunting zone from Lopsiding. It is doing LESS of what is considered normal by others. By reducing options or completely eliminating them, brands can stand out and differentiate themselves.

Withholding can help us succeed and stand out. In *The Paradox of Choice*, Barry Schwartz explains that when we have too many choices, we struggle to make decisions. He encourages us to "learn to love constraints" because "as the number of choices we face increases, freedom of choice becomes a tyranny of choice. Routine decisions take so much time and attention that it becomes difficult to get through the day. In circumstances like this, we should learn to view limits on the possibilities that we face as liberating not constraining."

Perhaps surprisingly, providing more options to customers can often paralyze them. As Erich Fromm explained in *Escape from Freedom*, "People are beset not by a lack of opportunity but by a dizzying abundance of it." It is counterintuitive, but limitations, not options, are what liberate customers.

Similarly, behavioral economist, Dan Ariely, in *Predictably Irrational*, argues that the common strategy of "keeping our options open" is a bad one and that we should "consciously start closing" some of those options. This is true because "they draw energy and commitment" away from activities that promise greater success.

One of the most common brand goals is growth. Get bigger. Make more money, open more locations, hire more employees, and increase sales. But some brands deliberately shrink or maintain their small size. They resist the pressure to expand. They stay small on purpose. Bo Burlingham profiles these unique companies in his book, *Small Giants: Companies that Choose to be Great Instead of Big.* Anchor Brewing and Zingerman's are two of the small giants.

Anchor Brewing in San Francisco was in the middle of an IPO. They were raising necessary capital to fuel their growth when the owner, Fritz Maytag, decided that he didn't want to get bigger. They didn't continue with the IPO. As Maytag explained, "This is not going to be a giant company… on my watch."

Zingerman's Deli is another example from *Small Giants*. They are an institution in Ann Arbor, Michigan. Customers loved the food so much that nationwide expansion seemed like the obvious next step. They could have been the next McDonald's, Subway, or Chipotle. But they took a different approach and focused on their local area, creating Zingerman's Community of Businesses. Instead of getting bigger, they got better and helped other business get better as well with financial and management support. The deli and the other businesses earn more than $50 million per year.[19]

David Rendall experiences the pressure to grow on a regular basis. As a speaker, he works on his own with no employees. He has no plans to grow, other than doing more speeches. He doesn't want to offer other services or expand into other businesses.

When people find this out, they regularly tell him that speaking doesn't scale. In other words, you can't grow it into a billion-dollar business like Amazon or Tesla. Additionally, David's business is dependent on his presence to deliver the speech. Businesses that scale can become independent of the founder and can generate income without the founder's ongoing involvement. All of that is true, to some extent, but it misses the point.

David doesn't want to scale his business. David wants to work by himself and for himself. David doesn't want to manage employees. David doesn't want to run a business. David wants to speak. That's what he enjoys. That's what he's good at doing.

---

19. http://chrisyeh.blogspot.com/2006/07/book-summary-small-giants.html

Additionally, a small business is a good fit for his other goals. Being a small business allows him time to spend with his family and to train extensively for Ironman triathlons and other endurance races. It's less money and fame but more of what matters to him. As Dan Pink says in *Free Agent Nation*, "Bigger isn't better. Better is better."

Withholding isn't just about size. You can do less in almost any area of your business. Let's look at four other examples.

1. **Chick-fil-A and Sundays** – 7-Eleven takes its name from its original every day operating hours. The company pioneered the convenience store concept, capitalizing on the fact that most grocery stores were closed on Sundays. In the next 25 years, most retail establishments, including restaurants, followed suit and are now open seven-days a week with longer hours. Many are even open on major holidays like Thanksgiving.

Chick-fil-A bucks this trend. The restaurant is primarily known for being a mall-based fast-food chain. They first opened in Hapeville, Georgia, in 1946. Chick-fil-A's founder, Truett Cathy made the conscious decision to be closed on Sundays.

According to QPolitical[20], the reason was practical as much as it was spiritually based. "Not only do they close on Sunday so believers can worship, they also want to make sure that [employees] have time to spend with [their] family. Not many companies care that much about their employees and it's refreshing to see one that truly does care." The simple act of being closed on Sunday has become a true differentiator for the brand.

Chick-fil-A is so popular, especially in the South, that they've been the subject of adoring songs, videos, and comedy routines created by raving fans. Their chicken, lemonade, and sweet tea are a religion and an addiction for many customers. Many people simply

---

20. http://www.qpolitical.com/real-reason-chick-fil-closes-sunday-will-blow-mind/

can't live without Chick-fil-A. It would seem then that the company is leaving a lot of money on the table by refusing to add Sunday hours.

Would they be more successful if they were open on Sundays? That's hard to say. However, in 2012 Chick-fil-A had the highest sales per store of any fast food chain at $3.1 million per store. In 2013, their total sales moved past KFC.

There's an old saying that "absence makes the heart grow fonder." Maybe Chick-fil-A builds up some anticipation, and desperation, by being closed on Sunday. It would be interesting to see if their Monday morning sales spike due to pent up demand.

Sometimes a pink goldfish doesn't go to work on Sunday.

2. **Lululemon sizing** – Lululemon Athletica was founded in Vancouver, British Columbia, by Chip Wilson in 1998. Although they offer a wide range of high-end athletic apparel for men and women, they are most famous for their women's yoga pants that cost just under $100.

It is relatively common for clothing retailers to offer options for a wide range of shapes and sizes. In contrast, Lululemon made a strategic decision in 2013 that they wouldn't sell plus-size clothing. Specifically, they would only offer yoga pants in size 12 and under. This was a very controversial decision that was widely covered in the media and has made them very unpopular with some customers and consumer advocacy groups (Antagonizing). Despite this criticism, they've maintained the policy. During a 2018 search of their website, we were unable to find any athletic pants above size 12 available. In some instances, a size 14 was listed, but was "sold out online."

Lululemon explained their reasoning[21] this way. "Our product and design strategy is built around creating products for our target guest in our size range of 2-12. While we know that doesn't work for everyone and recognize fitness and health come in all shapes and sizes, we've built our business, brand and relationship with our guests on this formula."

They acknowledge that their strategy limits the range of customers they can serve, and they are comfortable with that. "We want to be excellent at what we do, so this means that we can't be everything to everybody and need to focus on specific areas."[22]

Sometimes a pink goldfish gets so big that it can't buy pants from Lululemon.

3. **In-N-Out Burger** – Harry and Esther Snyder opened the first In-N-Out Burger in California in 1948. They currently have more than 300 locations along the West coast, and their fans are absolutely obsessed.

What makes In-N-Out unique is their intentionally limited menu. It looks like something from the 1950s, and it is. The menu hasn't changed much in the last 70 years. There are just four basic options: burgers, fries, shakes, and fountain drinks. They don't offer chicken or fish or onion rings or kid's meals or cookies or breakfast or many of the other items you can get from most fast food chains.

21. https://www.huffingtonpost.com/2013/08/02/lululemon-plus-size-clothing_n_3696690.html

22. http://blomedry.com/about-blo-blow-dry-bar/

Another way they withhold is with information. They have a secret menu of foods and options you can order that aren't on the official menu. For example, you can order up to four burger patties and four slices of cheese. It used to be unlimited until Tony Hsieh and his friends[23] in Las Vegas ordered 100 patties and 100 slices of cheese, and ruined it for the rest of us. You can also get your burger and/or fries "animal style," which includes specially grilled patties, extra sauce, and extra pickles. When you arrive at In-N-Out for the first time, it's unlikely you would know about these choices.

In-N-Out's unusually short menu is beneficial in a couple ways. It enables them to provide very fast service because they don't have to make a wide variety of foods. Also, their food is good because they do a few things really well. They are focused. Additionally, their secret menu gets people talking because it's fun to share a secret.

Sometimes a pink goldfish is an "animal style" burger.

4. **CVS quits smoking** – CVS was founded in 1963 as the Consumer Value Store in Massachusetts. Since then, they've become the biggest pharmacy chain in the U.S. They were ranked 7th on the Fortune 500 list in 2017. Their closest competitor is Walgreens, ranked 37th.

In 2014, CVS diverged from other pharmacy chains when they stopped selling cigarettes and other tobacco products in their stores. Their rationale was simple. Pharmacies exist to restore people's health. Tobacco products harm people's health.

They didn't just quit selling cigarettes. They also studied the response to this change by researching cigarette sales from other outlets after CVS exited the market. In areas where CVS had significant market share, there was a one percent reduction overall in cigarette sales.

---

23. http://whatupwilly.blogspot.com/2006/01/in-n-out-100x100.html

This is equal to the average smoker purchasing five fewer packs. That doesn't sound like a lot, but it adds up to more that 95 million packs overall. At the same time, CVS found a four percent increase in nicotine patch sales, which seems to show that there was a positive effect on smokers' habits.

CVS got a tremendous amount of attention for their surprising refusal to sell a product their customers were literally addicted to. They were featured in every major and many minor media outlets and received millions of dollars in free publicity.

As you probably noticed, their decision to stop selling tobacco is also polarizing. It will make them unpopular with cigarette smokers, but, at the same time, it has made them more popular with everyone else. We talked about this in the last chapter on Antagonizing. It is also an example of Opposing, which we will discuss in Chapter 11. When CVS stopped selling cigarettes, every other similar store was selling them. CVS did the opposite of everyone else.

Sometimes a pink goldfish doesn't smoke.

The W in F.L.A.W.S.O.M. is for Withholding, doing less. Let's move on to the S...

CHAPTER 10

SWERVING

"Without deviation progress is not possible."

- Frank Zappa

THE S IN F.L.A.W.S.O.M. STANDS FOR SWERVING

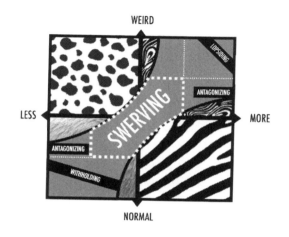

Swerving is about deviating, diverging, and veering. The emphasis here is on relatively small differentiation efforts. After reading about Flaunting, Lopsiding, Avoiding, and Withholding, it's easy to feel like differentiation requires massive changes to your brand or strategy. That's not always true. Sometimes you just need to turn a little bit to get away from the herd.

It's very common for brands to homogenize. As we look at what successful companies are doing, it's natural to emulate them. This has even been institutionalized in the process of benchmarking. We try to find out what others are doing right and then do the same thing. It sounds reasonable, but there's a problem.

When everyone in an industry starts copying the leaders, then, over time, the entire industry starts to look the same, feel the same, and sound the same. There are no differences. Nothing distinguishes one brand from another. It's herds of cows and zebras, and everyone's competing to be even more like the competition. As Youngme Moon explains in *Different - Escaping the Competitive Herd*, "The dynamic is not unlike a popularity contest in which everyone tries to win by being equal parts friendly, happy, active, and fun. Or an election campaign in which all the candidates try to be charming, serious, humble, and strong. Once everyone starts doing it, no one stands out." It's a downward spiral of conformity, a veritable sea of sameness.

If you want to stop the spiral, you don't have to run away at full speed. You can simply take a step in a different direction. It doesn't have to be the opposite direction—we'll get to that in the next chapter—just a different direction. You don't have to turn completely around, just a little to the right or a little to the left, and then keep going. It's okay to go slowly—just make sure to start going, start swerving.

One last note. Swerving is a good place to start before committing everything to a massive overhaul of your organization. Experiment. Do a pilot. Start small.

Swerving occupies the middle of the flaunting zone. Swerving involves doing a little MORE of what makes you weak or weird and doing a little LESS of what is considered normal by others.

For the last three years, REI has closed its stores and its website on Black Friday. They call it #OptOutside. It was a purposeful move to separate itself from other retailers. Instead of hitting the mall, the company wants customers to hit the trail. They are encouraging their employees and customers to go for a hike. "We really want this to be a day when people are outdoors, spending time with their families," says Jerry Stritzke, REI's CEO.

According to reporting by the *Washington Post*[24], industry analysts say they're seeing a [Black Friday] backlash as consumers realize

---

24. https://www.washingtonpost.com/news/business/wp/2017/10/30/
rei-thinks-you-have-better-things-to-do-than-shop-on-black-friday/

they can often get the same discounts days or weeks later without having to rush out on a holiday. "Black Friday has lost its significance," says Steven J. Barr, consumer markets leader for PwC. "Retailers have conditioned the consumer to believe everything's on sale every day, which means the deals on Black Friday are not significantly different from any other time."

Roughly 35 percent of consumers who planned to shop during Thanksgiving week in 2017 said they would do so on Black Friday, down from 51 percent in 2016 and 59 percent the year before, according to consumer markets research from PwC. "Black Friday has gotten weaker and weaker," said Stritzke of REI. "It's becoming less important."

In 2015, when REI announced it would remain closed on Black Friday, it was regarded as a radical move in an industry that relies heavily on holiday shopping. And messing with Black Friday, which is historically the most lucrative day of the year for many retailers, seemed risky. But the swerve paid dividends. In 2017, REI expanded the #OptOutside campaign by creating an online search engine for people to find nearby opportunities for activities such as hiking, rowing, and rock climbing.

How has this deviation from traditional retailers affected their business? Sales, profits, and revenues keep increasing every year. Being closed on the biggest shopping day hasn't hurt them. Instead, it has helped them and maybe made the world a better place.

Sometimes a pink goldfish is an empty store on Black Friday.

A good way to think about Swerving is that it's a small step in the direction of a bigger, or more extreme, differentiation strategy. These next four companies are great examples of Swerving, and each of them illustrates how a brand can start toward one of the pink goldfish strategies. Spirit Airlines swerves toward Withholding. Voodoo Doughnuts swerves toward Antagonizing. Nurse Next Door swerves toward Lopsiding, and Sheetz swerves toward Opposing, which we'll explore in the next chapter.

1. **Spirit and a la carte pricing** – Spirit Airlines actually began as a trucking company in Michigan in 1964. They began shipping via air in the 1970s, added passenger service in 1980, and changed their name to Spirit Airlines in 1992. In a world of low-cost airlines, they are an ultra-low-cost airline.

Spirit pioneered an a la carte pricing model that includes a $3 charge for in-flight beverages and a $10 fee for printing a boarding pass at the service desk. Former CEO Ben Baldanza was proud of the fact that Spirit was the first airline to charge for a checked bag.

Spirit's restrictive policies and poor customer service have led to a tidal wave of complaints, but the company isn't apologizing or changing course. "Our complaints are statistically much higher," Baldanza admits, "but compared to the number of people traveling with us, it's a tiny drop in the ocean. We're the Wal-Mart or the McDonald's—not the Nordstrom's—of the airline industry," Baldanza says. "No one walks into McDonald's and gets disappointed when they don't see filet mignon on the menu."

Spirit withholds almost everything that customers expect, and only provides it for an additional fee. They also use sexual innuendo in their advertisements (featured in the introduction to this book), which is offensive to some customers and an example of Antagonizing. Additionally, their lack of shame is a perfect illustration of Flaunting. Spirit Airlines is a pink goldfish all-star.

Sometimes a pink goldfish is an endless list of fees.

2. **Voodoo Doughnut and its unusual flavors** – Kenneth "Cat Daddy" Pogson and Tres Shannon founded Voodoo Doughnut in

Portland, Oregon, in 2003. They chose "voodoo" because they liked the number of O's in the word. This is obviously a very scientific approach to the branding process.

To set themselves apart from the standard doughnut shops of the world, the pair decided to create toppings in an entirely new way. Their maple doughnut is layered with two full strips of bacon. Other doughnuts are covered in Cap'n Crunch or Fruit Loops cereal. "We reinvented the doughnut shop," says Tres. "Everyone can say what they want, but no one was putting strips of bacon on a maple doughnut before us. No one was using cereal!"

Their signature doughnut is an edible voodoo doll. It's a plain doughnut with a face and arms and is covered with chocolate frosting and white decorations. A pretzel stick is included and can be used to stab the doll, which is filled with red jelly.

During shop hours, the pair experimented with new ingredients that began to turn heads. "The Nyquil doughnut really built up the hype around us," says Cat Daddy. "All of a sudden, we were on wacky morning radio talk shows all around the country. They talked about us on *The Wire*, Jay Leno mentioned us; it was madness,  especially for our first few months in business."

A doughnut covered in Pepto Bismol and crushed Tums was next. But both of the drug-laced doughnuts have been removed from the menu. The Portland Health Department determined that it wasn't safe for people to consume either one of the pharmaceutical pastries. Having your doughnut banned by a government agency definitely counts as Antagonizing.

If that wasn't enough, their Cock'N'Balls doughnut definitely antagonizes some visitors to their stores. We won't describe it for you here, but you can find a complete description on their website.

Voodoo Doughnut is also unusual in two other small ways. They only accept cash payments, and their signature pink boxes are famous worldwide. Additionally, you can see the "Keep Portland Weird" sign from the front of Voodoo Doughnut. They are definitely doing their part to fulfill that goal. We'll discuss weird places more in the final chapter.

Voodoo was submitted to the Pink Goldfish Project by Cody Goldberg.

Sometimes a pink goldfish is a Nyquil doughnut that is banned by the government.

3. **Nurse Next Door embraces happier aging** – Established in Vancouver in 2001, Nurse Next Door provides home healthcare services for senior citizens. You might remember their bright pink cars from Chapter 4. With competition in the home healthcare space intensifying, Nurse Next Door needed to stand out from its competitors with a brand refresh that portrays both the company and its clients as vibrant, fun-loving, and caring.

In 2017, the brand launched the Happier Aging campaign. Even though future clients were part of the Woodstock Generation, Arif Abdulla, VP of Global Franchise Development, says the industry still tends to present seniors in the wrong light. "We're an industry that's highly competitive, but also highly stale," he said. "If you look at our industry, it's filled with clinical, stale, muted imagery that doesn't really portray seniors in the way they see themselves." To combat this, the brand hired a full-time photographer/videographer for its team.[25]

The brand believes that aging is something to be celebrated. "Happier Aging" means reconnecting seniors with interests, hobbies, and passions that might have gotten lost amid busy schedules, health concerns, or other distractions.

One of the videos in the Happier Again campaign is a video[26] of a Nurse Next Door Care Designer named Stephanie. She talks about working with Miss Daisy, a wheelchair-bound senior in her mid 80's, to write her bucket list. The first item describes how Miss Daisy missed gardening. Stephanie helped her establish a tabletop garden.

The second item on her list was a bit more risqué. Miss Daisy wanted to see a male stripper. Stephanie says on the video, "Why not! Happier Aging is about living your life and having no boundaries." After receiving permission from her son, the caregiver brought Miss Daisy to *Thunder Down Under*. Miss Daisy had a wonderful time.

Sometimes a pink goldfish is a man in a thong.

4. **Sheetz and MTO** – Sheetz[27] is a family-owned Mid-Atlantic chain with more than 500 stores and 17,500 employees. The company is an innovator in convenience store customer experience. In 1986, Sheetz coined the term Made-to-Order, or "MTO." It's the ordering system that allows the store to prepare made-to-order sandwiches for customers. It took the stigma away from a "gas station sandwich" and transformed the business.

---

25. http://marketingmag.ca/brands/nurse-next-door-revamps-brand-image-39099/
26. https://www.youtube.com/watch?v=N7YyiSJrw5I
27. https://www.sheetz.com/

In 1986, Earl Springer was a store manager at a Sheetz in Williamsport, Maryland. His store was one of five in the chain to be a test case for selling fried chicken. Earl found that sales for chicken were great in warm weather, but they precipitously dropped off in the cold. The chicken also took 20 minutes to make and had limited shelf life. With sales dropping in January and an impending store visit from the President, Earl needed a new idea to stimulate sales.[28]

He and his team of sixteen employees brainstormed ways to jump start business. They set their focus on the store's pre-made deli offerings. Subs weren't doing well, selling less than a hundred sandwiches per week. The team figured the problem was one of perception. In the words of Clark Griswold in the 1983 movie *Vacation*[29], "I'm so hungry I could eat a sandwich from a gas station."

They started to pursue the concept of Made-to-Order (MTO) sandwiches[30]. The team visited two local sub stores for research. Earl determined they would avoid cheaper and focus on better. True to the mission of Sheetz, they'd provide quality customization to give customers what they wanted, when they wanted it. His team broke into groups to tackle menu, training, accounting, and marketing. One hurdle was convincing corporate leadership to fund a $1,100 sandwich preparation unit Earl had located. After getting the green light, the team experienced a slow start the first week. Undaunted, Earl and the team leaned in to market the new offering.

Signs, stickers, and radio station drops created awareness both in-store and within the community. It worked. Sub sales went from 96 pre-mades to 350 made-to-order subs per week and continued to climb. From there Earl helped Sheetz roll out MTO (Made to Order), retrofitting and retraining every store over the next few years. By the 1990s, MTO was a sales leader for Sheetz. Continuing

---

28. https://www.forbes.com/pictures/57290abe4bbe6f123f282d98/how-to-overcome-a-poor-ye/

29. https://www.youtube.com/watch?v=rvQPHGzVrlY

30. https://www.forbes.com/sites/stanphelps/2016/08/19/sheetz-redefined-the-convenience-store-customer-experience-with-mto/

to innovate, Stan Sheetz introduced touchscreen ordering for MTO in 1996. The picture-based system increased efficiency and allowed for greater accuracy. The introduction of MTO has not only had a huge impact on Sheetz but also on the entire convenience industry as a whole. The industry is now moving toward offering fresh food at a faster rate than ever.

Sheetz is similar to other gas stations and convenience stores in a lot of ways, but their made-to-order sandwiches are a small thing that helps them stand out.

Sometimes a pink goldfish is a gas station sandwich.

The S in F.L.A.W.S.O.M. is for Swerving, small deviations. Let's move on to the O...

CHAPTER 11

OPPOSING

*"Be fearful when others are greedy,
and be greedy when others are fearful."*

-Warren Buffett

THE "O" IN F.L.A.W.S.O.M. STANDS FOR OPPOSING

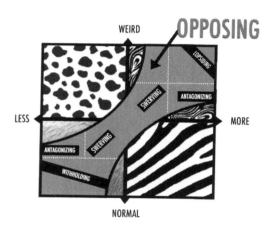

Opposing is doing the exact opposite of what others are doing. It's being unlike the competition. It's doing things that conflict with traditional methods.

Opposing brands are unlike other brands. They are contradictory, dissimilar. They operate in a way that is incompatible with everyone else. Opposing involves defying, resisting, and fighting. It's refusing to give in, to yield, to submit, to surrender to the pressure to conform, to fit in, to follow the crowd.

Opposing is simple. When everyone goes left, you go right. When everyone offers healthy options, you offer unhealthy ones. When everyone is open late, you close early.

This isn't like Swerving. It isn't a slight deviation from the norm. It's maximum separation. It's a complete break with convention.

It's worth taking a brief look at the definition of opposite. According to Dictionary.com[31], it means, "contrary or radically different in some respect common to both, as in nature, qualities, direction, result, or significance." This is interesting. To be opposites, two things need to be both very different and also have something in common. There's something that unites them but something else that completely separates them.

For example, being a tall person is the opposite of being a short person. Both are people, but they are opposites as it relates to height. However, being a tall person isn't the opposite of being a fat person. They are both people, but height and weight are just different qualities, not opposites. Fat and skinny are opposites. There has to be a similar method of comparing things for them to be opposites, and they also have to maintain some similarities.

So what? Why does this matter? It's important, because everything doesn't have to be different in order to be an opposite. In fact, if everything is different when you compare two things, they're not opposites. They are unrelated.

In other words, you don't have to leave your industry to do the opposite of what everyone else in your industry does. That's not doing the opposite. That's just joining or creating a different industry. Paradoxically, you have to maintain some similarities in order to be considered opposites.

For example, they sell socks in stores. You sell them online. They charge for shipping. You provide free shipping. They sell socks in packs of six pairs. You sell them one pair at a time. They sell long socks. You sell short socks. These are all examples of doing the opposite.

---

31. http://www.dictionary.com/browse/opposite

If you start selling hats instead of socks, this isn't the opposite. It's just different. (Although it is the opposite in the sense that you are covering heads while they are covering feet. Opposite ends of the body.)

Opposing occupies the top of the flaunting zone, just to the right of the center line. Brands here are fully embracing what makes them weird or weak. When everyone goes in one direction with the herd, opposing brands do the exact opposite.

Warren Buffett is one of the richest and most generous people in the world. He explained his formula for success in a *New York Times* article written during the spectacular meltdown of the financial sector in 2008. Buffett shares that his mantra is to do the opposite of what everyone else is doing. When everyone else zigs, he zags. Avoiding the crowd is what Opposing is all about.

Michael Lewis wrote *The Big Short* to tell the story of the few people who predicted and prepared for the crash of the sub-prime mortgage industry. One of the people he profiled was Mike Burry, a neurologist in California who has Asperger's syndrome, a form of autism. Burry's investment company, Scion Capital, had returns of 490 percent from 2000 to 2008, when the Standard and Poor's 500 returned only two percent during that same period.

Burry saw the demise of the real estate sector as early as 2005 and made nearly a billion dollars when it imploded. When asked to explain his special insight and willingness to go against the grain, he credited his success to the example of Warren Buffett. Burry believes that "to succeed in a spectacular fashion you have to be spectacularly unusual." We miss out on spectacular success when we are unwilling to be spectacularly unusual.

Let's take a closer look at Opposing with four examples of spectacularly unusual companies.

1. Tinder doesn't help you find "the one" – eHarmony is an on-line dating company that uses detailed profiles and matching software to help people find their soulmate. They advertise their success in creating more marriages than any other service. They help people find "the one" forever.

In contrast, Tinder uses simple profile photos to help people hook up with someone tonight. They don't help people find "the one" forever. They help people find someone right now. Both eHarmony and Tinder are successful companies, but they are opposites. It's not that one is succeeding and the other is failing. They are both effectively accomplishing different goals for different customers. Doing the opposite doesn't mean that what you are opposing is bad, ineffective, or unsuccessful.

Sometimes a pink goldfish is a swipe to the right.

2. Little Missmatched sells socks in sets of three – Little Missmatched sells socks that don't match, and they do it on purpose. The company was founded in 2004 with the goal of "disrupting the marketplace by reinventing a category." Their values include individuality and empowerment for girls.

Normal socks are sold in pairs. Each sock in the pair matches the other one. That is how socks work. Every year, people spend millions of hours on laundry trying to match their socks. Every year, millions of socks are lost, leaving a single sock with no matching partner.

But what if socks didn't need to match? David's friend Kenan wears mismatched socks. I asked him why and he explained that he doesn't like to waste time matching socks. When he folds clothes, he just combines the first two socks he finds into a pair.

Little Missmatched opposes the norm by selling socks in sets of three, none of which match each other. They also encourage girls to be unique by wearing distinctive socks that don't conform to traditional ideas of how they should dress. They tell girls they have the right to "not be like everyone else" and to show off their "kooky personality." They show girls that it can be fun to do the opposite of what everyone else is doing.

Sometimes a pink goldfish is three socks that don't match.

3. **The Barkley Marathons don't want you to finish** – In 1977, James Earl Ray, convicted of assassinating Martin Luther King Jr., escaped from prison in the mountains of Tennessee. After 55 hours, he was found just eight miles away. "Lazarus" Cantrell thought he could have gone at least 100 miles in the time it took Ray to go just eight. He couldn't, but this gave him an idea for a race, named after his friend Barry Barkley, in the same rugged environment.

It turns out that professional athletes can't run 100 miles over the brutal terrain either. Only 15 of 800 runners have completed the course since the race was started in 1986. In 2006, 30 of the 40 participants were unable to even complete the first two miles.

Let's look at how the Barkley Marathons are the opposite of normal races.

Normal marathons have a clear online registration process. The Barkley Marathons have no clear registration process. If you want to race, you need to mail a letter to the race organizer and hope he responds.

Normal marathons use timing chips to track runners on the course and as they finish. The Barkley Marathons have no electronic timing. Runners collect pages from paperback books at various milestones along the way to prove they've completed the course. For example, if you are runner #22, you rip out page #22 from the book at each checkpoint and bring it back with you in a plastic bag to the finish line.

Normal marathons provide course markers and maps as well as volunteers to clearly guide runners. The Barkley Marathons do not have a marked course. There is only one map. The course changes each year. You can't take the official map with you, but you can make one for yourself. Each time you finish a lap—there are five 20-mile laps—you have to do the next lap in the opposite direction, just to make navigation that much more difficult.

Normal marathons offer aid stations with drinks, snacks, water, ice, and medical care. The Barkley Marathons have no aid stations or volunteers or any assistance of any kind. Runners are on their own. They have to provide all supplies and carry everything with them.

Normal marathons charge a fee of around $100 to cover expenses or to donate to charity. The Barkley Marathons charge an application fee of $1.60. Participants also have to bring Lazarus, the race organizer, a license plate from their state/country and an additional "fee" that changes from year to year. One year it was a pack of tube socks. Another year it was a button-down shirt in the race organizer's size.

Normal marathons provide a clear start time for the race. The Barkley Marathons have no set start time. A race starts an hour after the race organizer blows the conch shell. It officially starts when he lights his cigarette.

Normal marathons have major corporate sponsors and advertising throughout the course. The Barkley Marathons have no sponsors and no advertising.

The Barkley Marathon is so unusual and so interesting that it was the subject of a very popular Netflix documentary. It is one of the most desirable races for endurance runners throughout the world.

Sometimes a pink goldfish a race that you can't sign up for and couldn't finish anyway.

4. **Patagonia doesn't want you to buy their clothes** – Most clothing retailers want you to buy their clothes. In fact, they spend a tremendous amount of time and money trying to convince you to visit their stores and buy their stuff. That's why it was surprising when Patagonia placed an ad in *The New York Times* telling people not to buy one of their jackets. Patagonia paid money on Black Friday for an opportunity to push people away from their stores on the biggest shopping day of the year.

Patagonia is so serious about sustainability and environmental responsibility that they want customers to think twice before buying new clothes. The company explained their reasoning this way.

"It's part of our mission to inspire and implement solutions to the environmental crisis. It would be hypocritical for us to work for environmental change without encouraging customers to think before they buy. To reduce environmental damage, we all have to reduce consumption as well as make products in more environmentally sensitive, less harmful ways.... It's folly to assume that a healthy economy can be based on buying and selling more and more things people don't need—and it's time for people who believe that's folly to say so."

Their goal is to create products that last longer and are replaced less often. In this way, they can stay in business and stay true to their values. But they need cooperation from consumers in order to make their vision a reality.

Worn Wear[32] is another way that Patagonia is doing the opposite of most clothing retailers. They buy back used Patagonia clothing, clean and repair it, and then resell it.

"Worn Wear is a set of tools to help our customers partner with Patagonia to take mutual responsibility to extend the life of the products Patagonia makes and customers purchase. The program provides significant resources for responsible care, repair, reuse and resale, and recycling at the end of a garment's life."

Sometimes a pink goldfish is a used jacket.

The O in F.L.A.W.S.O.M. is for Opposing, doing the opposite. Let's move on to the M...

32. https://hypebeast.com/2017/9/patagonia-worn-wear-launch

CHAPTER 12

MICRO-WEIRDING

"You need to understand the market, know how you can differentiate yourself in it, and grasp the functional differentiation competitive points that are going to allow you to be disruptive."

- Audrey MacLean

THE "M" IN F.L.A.W.S.O.M. STANDS FOR MICRO-WEIRDING

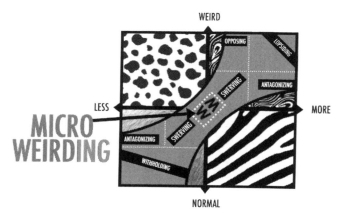

Micro-weirding is using miniscule actions to differentiate your brand. This chapter includes minute examples that don't necessarily have a category but were too good to leave out of the book. The lesson is that you can set your brand apart without some cohesive master plan; you can be just a tiny bit weird.

And just because something is micro-weird, doesn't mean it has a micro-impact. The examples in this chapter will show how itty-bitty actions can having a massive impact on your brand.

Micro-weirding occupies the heart of the flaunting zone. Micro-weirding is doing very small things to stand out. This is the easiest and least risky way to begin creating your pink goldfish. If you wanted to organize the types in phases, they would look like this.

- Phase 1: Micro-weirding (low weirdness)

- Phase 2: Swerving (moderate weirdness)

- Phase 3: Lopsiding & Withholding (high weirdness)

- Phase 4: Opposing & Antagonizing (massive weirdness)

In 2009, Stan started searching for companies who purposely put an emphasis on the customer experience by practicing the art of lagniappe. Lagniappe is a creole word that originated in the 1840s in Louisiana. A mix of French and Spanish, it means "the gift" or "to give more." In New Orleans, it was customary for a merchant to do a little something extra at the time of purchase. It was something that was added beyond the transaction to honor the relationship. Any time someone does a little something extra in Louisiana, that's lagniappe.

Lagniappe is not to be confused with the extra in a baker's dozen. To truly understand a baker's dozen[33], we need to travel back to its origin in England over 800 years ago. The term dates back to the 13th century during the reign of Henry III. During this time, there was a perceived need for regulations to control quality and check weights to avoid fraudulent activity. The Statute of Bread and Ale was instituted to regulate the sale of bread and beer.

Bakers who violated the law could be liable for severe punishment such as losing a hand by the blow of an axe. To guard against the punishment, the baker would give 13 for the price of 12 to be certain of not being known as a cheat. The merchants created the "baker's dozen" concept to change customer perception. They understood that one of the 13 loaves could be lost, eaten, burnt, or ruined in some way and still leave the baker with the original legal dozen. The irony of the Baker's Dozen is that it's not based in the idea of giving a little unexpected extra to the customer to stand out. It was about insurance and covering one's backside for fear of losing a hand.

---

33. http://en.wikipedia.org/wiki/Baker%27s_dozen

A CONSCIOUS CHOICE

Micro-weirding is differentiation by experience design. A marketing investment back into your customers so to speak. It's that unexpected surprise that's thrown in for good measure to achieve differentiation, drive retention, and promote word of mouth. After crowd sourcing over 1,001 examples of lagniappe, Stan published *Purple Goldfish* in 2012. This chapter is our way of offering a little something extra to you by sharing examples of companies that do something a little weird. Here are 11 examples. Why 11? We'll dial that up in Chapter 15.

1. Not your ordinary Joe – Joseph Coulombe conceived an idea for a supermarket while vacationing in the Caribbean. He opened his first store in Pasadena in 1967. Coulombe noticed that as Americans began to travel more, the ability to purchase those foreign foods and wines they enjoyed while traveling was a challenge when they returned home. His name and a South Seas motif became the inspiration for Trader Joe's. Today, the company has nearly 500 stores in 43 states and Washington, D.C.

Beyond the staff wearing Caribbean shirts, when it comes to embracing weirdness and providing a good customer service experience, Trader Joe's understands the importance of taking care of the customer. While the customer base itself is not made up of children, it is made up of many people who have children. Trader Joe's has not ignored that—in fact, they've embraced it since their founding. In addition to offering a variety of free samples, they also have a stuffed whale and miniature shopping carts. As for the stuffed whale, if you find it, your child gets a treat out of a treasure box and then you get to hide the whale yourself for others to find.

Sometimes a pink goldfish is a miniature shopping cart.

2. Popsicles by the pool – When was the last time you had a popsicle? Not recently. When was the last time you had a popsicle at a hotel? You probably haven't. When was the last time you had a popsicle delivered to you at a hotel? Probably never. Have you ever complained because popsicles weren't on the room service menu? Probably not.

So why would a hotel create a popsicle hotline and why would anyone care? In their book, *The Power of Moments*, the Heath brothers categorize the popsicle hotline as a "peak" moment. They argue that people value and remember small unusual moments more than larger, seemingly more important, services.

This seems to be true for the Magic Castle Hotel, the highest-rated hotel in the Los Angeles area according to TripAdvisor. "Out of over 3,000 reviews on TripAdvisor[34], 94% of guests rate the hotel as either 'excellent' or 'very good.'"

But why are the ratings so high? Wouldn't people rather stay at a consistently luxurious property like the Four Seasons? The Magic Castle Hotel doesn't have an amazing pool or beautiful furniture or lovely rooms. It doesn't have most of the things that you'd expect from a great hotel.

What it does have is a Popsicle Hotline. Here's how it works. There's a red phone on a wall by the pool. When you lift the handset, a popsicle specialist answers and takes your order. You don't have to wait long until an employee wearing white gloves brings your popsicles on a silver tray at no charge.

As the Heath brothers explain, "What the Magic Castle has figured out is that, to delight customers, you need not obsess over every detail. Customers will forgive small swimming pools and underwhelming room décor, as long as you deliver some magical peak

---

34. https://www.tripadvisor.com/Hotel_Review-g32655-d84502-Reviews-Magic_Castle_Hotel-Los_Angeles_California.html

moments. The surprise about great service experiences is that they are mostly forgettable." In other words, being micro-weird can be a very valuable differentiation strategy, especially when everyone else is trying to be good at everything.

Sometimes a pink goldfish is a red popsicle phone.

3. Peppercomm thinks comedy training is good for business – Steve Cody is one of Peppercomm's founders. He was taking stand-up comedy classes in the evening and his team noticed it was helping him at work. As he got better at comedy, his presentations also got better.

He decided that if it was helping him, it might help others. Initially, the whole Peppercomm management team was exposed to the comedic curriculum. The results were so positive that the training filtered down through the entire organization. Now all employees are required to take the training when they are hired, even interns.

Comedy is credited with making employees better listeners, improving teamwork, increasing productivity, and making work more enjoyable. Humor infuses the company's internal emails and external client communication. They've even started offering the training to current and prospective clients.

Sometimes a pink goldfish is a manager who does stand-up comedy.

4. Aztec Secret lives up to its name – Aztec Secret Indian Healing Clay is one of Amazon's best-selling beauty products, but if you're trying to find the product's founder, it's going to be difficult. Unlike a lot of famous founders and CEOs, she is abnormally anonymous. Is she hiding or is she just busy?

Even though people can't find her, they can definitely find her product. Aztec Secret is always in the top ten in the list of Amazon's beauty bestsellers, and it has more than 10,700 positive reviews.

Unlike most beauty products, this secret clay isn't fancy or expensive. It is sold by the pound for just $10 and has just one ingredient, bentonite powder. The packaging appears to have been designed in 1973.

Aztec doesn't advertise. Their first website didn't list an email address or a street address, just a PO box. When people contact the company for interviews, they are asked to send a request via fax but no one seems to respond.

The product was initially sold in health food stores. The first Amazon reviews started in 2005 and began to accelerate in 2008. It isn't clear exactly how and when the product became so popular, especially without the use of traditional advertising or social media.

An enterprising and relentless journalist managed to discover that Aztec is the creation of Mary Roman and was started in 1986. Apparently, her children now run the business but no one can find them either.

Sometimes a pink goldfish is a well-kept secret.

5. **Assurance loves old pop songs** – According to Steven Handmaker, CMO at Assurance, culture is the secret sauce at this insurance brokerage. Each year they rally around a theme and an accompanying song. The songs are typically from the 1980's with a fun/irreverent feel. In 2017, it was the "Power of Love" by Huey Lewis. The previous year was Salt-N-Pepa's "Push It" and the theme was wellness. Their Shared Success bonus program is based on four components (two financial and two that tie in with the cultural theme). For example, during the wellness year, everyone in the company would achieve success if 84% of the company completed a 5K race at some point during the year. Over 95% ended up doing completing a 5K race. In 2017, the metric was handwritten notes of which 20 were meant for customers and 17 for friends/family. Over

the last few years, Assurance has become a fixture on *Fortune's* Best Place to Work (for Small to Medium businesses) and won "Best Place to Work in Chicago" awarded by the *Chicago Tribune*. Not bad for a boring insurance brokerage.

Sometimes a pink goldfish is basing your annual strategy on a song from the 1980s.

6. **Liberty Tax and its wavers** – Accountants are professionals. Taxes are serious business. No one wants to mess with the IRS. That's why it's surprising that Liberty Tax hires wavers to dress up like the Statue of Liberty and sing and dance and wave at the people driving by.

It started accidentally. A Liberty Tax franchise was recording a commercial. During the filming, a costumed actor waved to people and the people waved back. The story made it back to the corporate headquarters, and the marketing department decided to try wavers on a larger scale.

You might think that being a waver is a simple entry-level job and anyone could do it. That is not the case. Potential wavers have to try out for the job. After demonstrating their moves outside, only the best ones are hired.

Wavers dressed up like Lady Liberty are weird, but do they actually impact the business? Liberty's Chief Marketing Officer, Martha O'Gorman, has statistics to show that wavers work. She cites increased brand recognition for Liberty—they're competitive with H&R Block—as a sign that taxpayers pay attention to the wavers.

Sometimes a pink goldfish is a green statue with a crown.

7. **Dropping the sticky bomb** – Joe Sorge opened the Milwaukee restaurant AJ Bombers in 2009, self-described as "Rube Goldberg meets Willy Wonka and the Chocolate factory. Except Rube is into

P-nuts and Willy Wonka is into crazy Cheeseburgers. And both are very happy about it." One of the micro-weird things is free peanuts for patrons. If you are sitting at a booth, they are shot at you with metal WWII bombers. It doesn't end there. Here are three more signature elements of micro-weirdness from the restaurant:

- **Oversize beach chairs** – a couple of larger than life beach chairs. You feel like a silly little kid while sitting (but isn't that the point).

- **Quad cow** – take on the quad cow at AJ Bombers. After you've swallowed the last bite of your four-patty burger, you can sign your name on the sacred cow that adorns the wall.

- **Sharpies** – grab a marker and leave your name or Twitter handle on the wall. You are now part of AJ Bombers.

Sometimes a pink goldfish is a metal WWII bomber that delivers peanuts.

8. **Free ice cream or coffee** – Stew Leonard grew up the son of a dairy farmer who was in the milk delivery business. The 1960s brought a time of great change for his business. Two things would shake the core of the business. First, the demand for milk delivery was evaporating. Second, the State of Connecticut evoked eminent domain and furrowed the dairy farm to make room for a new highway called Route 7. Pivoting, Stew opened his first dairy store in Norwalk, Connecticut, in 1969. The 17,000 sq. ft. store sold only eight products.

During his first year in business, he was asked by the local elementary school to come out and speak on career day. The principal asked Stew to talk about his store and the dairy business. Even though Stew didn't see the appeal for kids, he reluctantly agreed. As Stew pulled into the parking lot, he knew he was in trouble. There was a fire truck parked in front of the school with kids all around it. It didn't get any better when he walked through the doors of the school. He immediately saw a room with an Air Force officer. A movie about the history of jet airplanes was playing. It was filled with kids. Across the hall was a police officer showing a packed classroom about various police equipment and weapons. He proceeded to walk down the hall and eventually found his classroom. There was a sign on the door that read "The Dairy Business." Stew entered the room to find only three kids sitting there. Two of whom were the sons of his produce manager. For the next 30 minutes he talked about the dairy business and running a store. At the end of the talk, he thanked the kids. Stew then reached into his pocket and handed them each a coupon for a free ice cream. The kids left and Stew waited to present the second of his two Career Day sessions. He waited and waited... no kids. More than 15 minutes passed, still no kids. After 20 minutes the principal came rushing in and exclaimed, "Stew... I don't know what you told those kids, but we have to move your next presentation to the school auditorium." This simple story underscores the impact of word of mouth with the power of a little micro-weirdness.

Today Stew Leonard's continues the tradition of free ice cream. Customers who purchase $100 or more in groceries get a free ice cream or cup of coffee. It's that little extra or "WOW" according to Stew that makes all the difference.

Sometimes a pink goldfish is a free ice cream cone.

9. **Rebecca Minkoff, Vincent, and the MAC** – Rebecca Minkoff has been designing coveted apparel, handbags, shoes, and accessories since she moved to New York City at the age of eighteen. Her MAC (morning after clutch) bags embrace a little micro-weirdness. They all have an extra business card in them. The card has a picture of an attractive man on the front. On the back there is a handwritten note that says "call me," signed by "Vincent" with a phone

number. According to Vanessa Khedouri who contributed the example, "When you call [give it a try at +1 (646) 420-1475], there is a recording of a message from "Vincent"—a guy with a sexy French accent. I love that touch and it feels personal!"

According to Rebecca Minkoff, "I find cute pics and have them printed on cards and people actually do call! When customers call, they hear a guy's voice and he is French. Some people call and think they met the guy the night before. It's kind of funny to hear some of the messages!"

Sometimes a pink goldfish is fictitious French guy named Vincent.

10. **A tinfoil swan and oyster shooters!** – Tucked under the Morrison Bridge in Portland, Le Bistro Montage opened its doors in 1992. With communal tables and late hours, the restaurant embraces micro-weirdness. Here are couple of Stan's favorites from the restaurant.

Oyster and Mussel Shooters – these slimy fellas are served in a shot glass with some cocktail sauce and horseradish. Once ordered, the waiter or waitress will immediately scream to the kitchen, "OYSTER SHOOOOOTER."

Your leftovers get wrapped up in tin foil. Move over balloon animal guy, the staff at the Bistro will "WOW" you with their animals like a tin foil swan. Here's the blog *Wandering Chopsticks*[35] commenting on the practice, "We could have easily finished our entrees but we saved some for leftovers just so we could have this! Leftovers wrapped inside a foil cat and mouse. Yes, I'm still a kid and get inordinate pleasure in seeing what shape my leftovers will come out in. Once, I even saw a foil Superman with upraised arms as if in flight and foil cape. And another time, a little kid gasped with delight when he got a foil sword that was longer than his arm."

---

35. http://wanderingchopsticks.blogspot.com/2009/06/le-bistro-montage-portland-oregon.html

Sometimes a pink goldfish is a foil sword of leftovers.

11. Izzy's Ice Cream and mini-scoops – Driven by a desire to run their own business and a genuine love for ice cream, Jeff and Lara Sommers opened the doors to Izzy's Ice Cream in 2000. Together they make more than 150 flavors of ice cream. One of the micro-weird things they do is sampling. For every scoop of ice cream purchased at Izzy's, the buyer gets a little mini-scoop on top for free. The little patented mini-scoop is called the Izzy. It's a little something extra for customers.

Sometimes a pink goldfish is a mini-scoop of ice cream.

The M in F.L.A.W.S.O.M. is for Micro-weirding, tiny oddities. Now let's examine how to bring your pink goldfish to life...

FOUR A'S
(THE HOW)

ASSESS

*"It's up to each of us alone to figure out
who we are, who we are not, and to act more
or less consistently with those conclusions."*

- Tom Peters

We shared categories of examples showing WHAT companies have done to differentiate themselves in the previous section.

This section explores HOW to apply these lessons in your organization.

In the next four chapters, we'll look at how you can *think differently* about your organization and then *act differently* in order to stand out from your competition.

Thinking differently involves Assessing (Chapter 13) and Appreciating (Chapter 14) your organization's flaws.

Acting differently includes Amplifying (Chapter 15) those flaws and then Aligning (Chapter 16) them with the right people, products, places, and positioning.

Let's start with Assess.

WHAT MAKES YOUR ORGANIZATION UNIQUE?

Being unique is about being different, being unusual, and being uncommon. Unfortunately, instead of embracing our uniqueness, we often try to hide it in an effort to be more normal. We tend to focus on the ways our businesses are similar to others. We've learned that benchmarking and emulating the success of other organizations is a proven path to success.

Because of this bias, it's helpful to spend some time thinking about what makes your company odd, atypical, and exceptional. To help with this process, we've designed a simple checklist of possible company characteristics.

Almost every strategic planning process begins with an analysis of the organization's strengths, weaknesses, opportunities, and threats (SWOT). We've designed an organizational assessment to help you see your organization's strengths and weaknesses in a new light.

TAKE THE ASSESSMENT

1. Put an X in the box on the left next for the positive characteristics of your organization, people, culture, and/or products and services.

2. If you notice any characteristics that are definitely not a strength, draw a line through them.

3. Choose your organization's top five strengths and rank them from one to five (one being the strongest).

X	Strengths		Rank
	1.	Large, Substantial	
	2.	Responsive, Quick	
	3.	Local, Familiar	
	4.	Global, Exotic	
	5.	Inexpensive	
	6.	Luxurious	
	7.	Activist, Revolutionary	
	8.	Conventional, Traditional	
	9.	Hand-crafted, Unique	
	10.	Standardized, Uniform	
	11.	Simple, Clean	
	12.	Intricate, Elaborate	
	13.	Automated, Programmed	
	14.	Personal, Individualized	
	15.	Disposable	
	16.	Permanent, Lasting	
	17.	Objective, Rational	

18.	Sensitive, Caring	
19.	Fun, Entertaining	
20.	Serious, Professional	
21.	Patient, Deliberate	
22.	Spontaneous, Instinctive	
23.	Reliable, Dependable	
24.	Exciting, High Performance	
25.	Fast Growing	
26.	Steady, Consistent Growth	
27.	New, Innovative	
28.	Reputable, Established	
29.	Cooperative, Friendly	
30.	Competitive, Assertive	
31.	Vigilant, Alert	
32.	Satisfied, Content	
33.	Systematic, Deliberate	
34.	Agile, Responsive	
35.	Focused, Specialized	
36.	Diversified	
37.	Lavish, Extravagant	
38.	Frugal, Thrifty	
39.	Cautious, Careful	
40.	Courageous, Audacious	
41.	Challenging, Stimulating	
42.	Agreeable, Conciliatory	
43.	Daring, Bold	
44.	Refined, Conservative	

Now, let's identify your organization's weaknesses. Here are the directions:

1. Put an X in the box on the left next to the weak areas of your organization, people, culture and/or products and services.

2. If you notice any characteristics that are definitely not a weakness, draw a line through them.

3. Choose your organization's top five weaknesses and rank them from one to five (one being the weakest).

X	Weaknesses		Rank
	1.	Bulky, Cumbersome	
	2.	Small, Weak	
	3.	Regular, Ordinary	
	4.	Foreign, Unfamiliar	
	5.	Cheap, Low Quality	
	6.	Expensive, Overpriced	
	7.	Rebellious, Radical	
	8.	Old-fashioned, Conformist	
	9.	Irregular, Rough	
	10.	Ordinary, Common	
	11.	Plain, Dull	
	12.	Complex	
	13.	Impersonal, Cold	
	14.	Labor-intensive, Unpredictable	
	15.	Poor quality, Shoddy	
	16.	Fixed, Unchanging	
	17.	Detached, Insensitive	

18.	Vulnerable, Emotional	
19.	Silly, Immature	
20.	Somber, Humorless	
21.	Slow, Indecisive	
22.	Impatient, Impulsive	
23.	Boring, Predictable	
24.	Unreliable, Inconsistent	
25.	Unstable, Volatile	
26.	Slow, Plodding	
27.	Untested, Unproven	
28.	Old, Outdated	
29.	Passive, Reactive	
30.	Aggressive, Hostile	
31.	Anxious, Fearful	
32.	Complacent, Ignorant	
33.	Bureaucratic, Inflexible	
34.	Reactive, Unpredictable	
35.	Limited, Restricted, Narrow	
36.	Unfocused, Scattered	
37.	Wasteful, Reckless	
38.	Stingy, Cheap	
39.	Fearful, Timid	
40.	Careless, Foolish	
41.	Confrontational, Demanding	
42.	Weak, Submissive	
43.	Irreverent, Offensive	
44.	Boring, Uninspiring	

NOW WHAT?

At this point, after completing the assessment of your organization's strengths and weaknesses, most business books would encourage you to use your newfound awareness to fix the weaknesses. That is the exact opposite of what we're going to recommend. We don't want you to fix your weaknesses. We want you to appreciate them by discovering that your organization's weaknesses are important clues to your organization's most powerful strengths.

CHAPTER 14

APPRECIATE

*"The notion that everyone can be everything
to everybody at all times, is completely off the mark."*

– Keith Ferrazzi

Once you know your company's strengths and weaknesses, what should you do? The conventional wisdom is to build on strengths and fix weaknesses. Don't appreciate. Instead, adjust and adapt. As you already know, we disagree with this approach because every weakness has a corresponding strength. So, let's build on the weaknesses instead. But it only makes sense to do that if we think differently and truly appreciate the value of our organization's flaws.

Appreciation is the second part of thinking differently about your organization. Appreciation is the essence of this book. It is seeing that your organization's flaws make it awesome. But that can be very difficult to do in an environment that provides more criticism than appreciation.

CRITICISM

The opposite of criticism is appreciation. Within our organizations most of us are more familiar with criticism than appreciation, especially when it comes to being unusual. As Alex Bogusky warns, "Life conspires to beat the rebel out of you."

Because of this external pressure to conform and to homogenize our organization's offerings, most companies try to find a way that pleases everyone or displeases no one. But it simply isn't possible to find an approach that makes all customers happy. Anything we do will end up alienating someone. If we believe that our company can please everyone by becoming perfect, by fixing all of our weaknesses, we will fail. For example, not everyone likes Starbucks or McDonald's or Apple or Wal-Mart, and yet they are very successful companies.

Our company's products or services can't make everyone happy, and it is futile to try. Frei and Morriss, in *Uncommon Service*, encourage managers to "decide what trade-offs you will make—where you will do things badly, even very badly, in the service of great." Success is about delighting the right customers and being willing to make other customers unhappy.

Celebrity chef Rachel Ray doesn't mind being criticized. "If you spend so much time thinking about the people who dislike what it is you're doing, you're doing a disservice to the people that employ you. I'm not employed by those people. I work for the people that want the type of food I write [about], the type of food we share with people."

One way to deal more effectively with criticism is to reframe it as a sign that you are doing something right. Sally Hogshead, author of *Fascinate*, argues that "if you're not eliciting a negative response from someone, then you're probably not very compelling to anyone." Being criticized, by at least some potential customers, means you are on the right track. In this way, criticism becomes a form of positive feedback or praise.

COMPARISON

Another barrier to appreciating our organization's flaws is comparison. When it comes to competition, it is tempting to compare our organization to others that seem more successful or more popular. We imagine that they have big strengths and no weaknesses. But this isn't true. As we'll see in this chapter, our organization's apparent weaknesses are also strengths, and the competition's obvious strengths are also weaknesses. We need to find ways to capitalize on our organization's unique characteristics and use our apparent flaws to our advantage.

In *Enemy of the State*, a conspiracy-theory thriller, Gene Hackman tries to help Will Smith evade government agents who are trying to capture him. Smith sees his situation as hopeless, but Hackman changes his perspective by offering a lesson in guerrilla warfare. "You use your weakness as strength. They're big and you're small. But that means they're slow and you're fast. They're exposed and you're hidden." He reframes the enemy's apparent strength (being big) as weakness (slow and exposed) and Smith's apparent weakness (being small) as strength (fast and hidden).

A great example of appreciation can be found in the discount retail industry. Wal-Mart's main strength is low prices, but its weaknesses include poor quality merchandise, long lines, and unhelpful employees. Meanwhile, Target's main strengths are higher quality products from well-known designers, attractive stores, and helpful associates who are quick to open a new checkout lane. However, Target's weakness is that its prices are not as low as those at Wal-Mart.

What would happen if, instead of appreciating them, Wal-Mart tried to fix their weaknesses? What would happen to their low prices, their primary strength, as they added better products and extra employees at the registers? The answer is simple. Their prices would climb, thus diminishing their strength.

What if Target decided to fix their weakness by lowering prices? What would happen to the level of customer service and the great products that give them their advantage if they focused more on cost cutting? Again, the answer is straightforward. Their quality and service would decrease, thus diminishing their strength.

For proof of this, look at Kmart. They provide an illustration of what happens when a company, or individual, loses focus and tries to fix weaknesses instead of focusing on strengths. Their historical leadership in discount retail was based on the blue-light special, a symbol of low prices. However, they did not focus exclusively on this price advantage and began to lose customers to Wal-Mart.

Kmart then began adding designer products from celebrities like Martha Stewart but wasn't quite ready to shed their low-price image. This allowed Target to capture higher-income customers who were design-conscious, while Wal-Mart attracted lower-income customers who were cost-conscious.

Kmart's efforts to fix their weaknesses ultimately led to bankruptcy. They became undifferentiated. They weren't the best at anything, so customers had no reason to shop there. Their failure illustrates the dangers of trying to eliminate weaknesses and be more well-rounded. As Harvard marketing professor Youngme Moon explains in her book, *Different*, "True differentiation is rarely a function of well-roundedness; it is typically a function of lopsidedness."

There is a compelling reason to go to Wal-Mart—low prices. There is a compelling reason to go to Target—better service and design. But there is no compelling reason to go to Kmart. Their prices aren't the lowest and their service and design aren't the best. They are just mediocre in both areas, so people don't shop there.

And it keeps getting worse. After going bankrupt, Kmart bought Sears. Now the combined company is facing bankruptcy again and closing stores throughout the country. In their attempt to be the best of both worlds, they've become the worst of both worlds.

This is crucial. When we try to fix organizational weaknesses, we often end up damaging the corresponding strengths. Our efforts to make our companies better can end up making them worse. As Frances Frei and Anne Morriss explain in *Uncommon Service*, "striving for all-around excellence leads directly to mediocrity."

It may seem like reframing is just denial, dishonesty, or spin control, but it's not. Each business has unique characteristics that have both positive and negative features. These features, which we usually refer to as strengths and weaknesses, cannot be separated. They come in pairs. The positive and negative elements are inextricably linked. It's common to believe that there's nothing strong about your particular weaknesses or the weaknesses of other businesses. However, every weakness has a corresponding strength.

Now let's look at the connections between your particular organization's strengths and weaknesses.

Transfer the top five strengths and top five weaknesses from the last chapter to the chart below. Look for connections between strengths and weaknesses. For example...

- Companies can be seen *negatively* as small and weak (2) or *positively* as quick and responsive (2)

- Products can be seen negatively as overpriced (6) or positively as luxurious (6)

- Services can be seen negatively as complex (12) or positively as intricate and elaborate (12)

Strengths		Weaknesses	
1.	Large, Substantial	1.	Bulky, Cumbersome
2.	Responsive, Quick	2.	Small, Weak
3.	Local, Familiar	3.	Regular, Ordinary
4.	Global, Exotic	4.	Foreign, Unfamiliar
5.	Inexpensive	5.	Cheap, Low Quality
6.	Luxurious	6.	Expensive, Overpriced
7.	Activist, Revolutionary	7.	Rebellious, Radical
8.	Conventional, Traditional	8.	Old-Fashioned, Conformist
9.	Hand-Crafted, Unique	9.	Irregular, Rough
10.	Standardized, Uniform	10.	Ordinary, Common
11.	Simple, Clean	11.	Plain, Dull
12.	Intricate, Elaborate	12.	Complex
13.	Automated, Programmed	13.	Impersonal, Cold
14.	Personal, Individualized	14.	Labor-intensive, Unpredictable
15.	Disposable	15.	Poor Quality, Shoddy
16.	Permanent, Lasting	16.	Fixed, Unchanging
17.	Objective, Rational	17.	Detached, Insensitive
18.	Sensitive, Caring	18.	Vulnerable, Emotional
19.	Fun, Entertaining	19.	Silly, Immature
20.	Serious, Professional	20.	Somber, Humorless
21.	Patient, Deliberate	21.	Slow, Indecisive
22.	Spontaneous, Instinctive	22.	Impatient, Impulsive
23.	Reliable, Dependable	23.	Boring, Predictable
24.	Exciting, High Performance	24.	Unreliable, Inconsistent
25.	Fast Growing	25.	Unstable, Volatile
26.	Steady, Consistent Growth	26.	Slow, Plodding
27.	New, Innovative	27.	Untested, Unproven

Strengths		Weaknesses	
28.	Reputable, Established	28.	Old, Outdated
29.	Cooperative, Friendly	29.	Passive, Reactive
30.	Competitive, Assertive	30.	Aggressive, Hostile
31.	Vigilant, Alert	31.	Anxious, Fearful
32.	Satisfied, Content	32.	Complacent, Ignorant
33.	Systematic, Deliberate	33.	Bureaucratic, Inflexible
34.	Agile, Responsive	34.	Reactive, Unpredictable
35.	Focused, Specialized	35.	Limited, Restricted, Narrow
36.	Diversified	36.	Unfocused, Scattered
37.	Lavish, Extravagant	37.	Wasteful, Reckless
38.	Frugal, Thrifty	38.	Stingy, Cheap
39.	Cautious, Careful	39.	Fearful, Timid
40.	Courageous, Audacious	40.	Careless, Foolish
41.	Challenging, Stimulating	41.	Confrontational, Demanding
42.	Agreeable, Conciliatory	42.	Weak, Submissive
43.	Daring, Bold	43.	Irreverent, Offensive
44.	Refined, Conservative	44.	Boring, Uninspiring

When you choose anything, you reject everything else.... So when you take one course of action, you give up all the other courses.
– G.K. Chesterton

The following stories show how seemingly obvious flaws actually conceal surprising strengths. These examples illustrate the unique relationship between strengths and weaknesses. It is our hope that they will move you from being ashamed of your weaknesses to intense appreciation for your apparent flaws.

Our strength grows out of our weakness.
- Ralph Waldo Emerson, Compensation

DISORGANIZATION

It's good to be neat and it's bad to be messy. At least that's what we're told. We've all heard that "cleanliness is next to godliness" and "a cluttered desk is a sign of a cluttered mind." Furthermore, most people believe that they would be happier and more successful if they were more organized. This desire is evidenced by the success of the Container Store and the endless list of television shows dedicated to cleaning up and reorganizing messy homes. Being disorganized seems like an obvious weakness that needs to be fixed. Right?

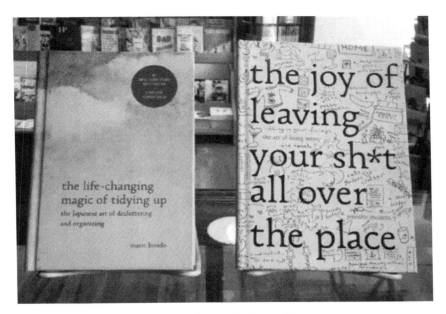

Photo Credit: Sizzle.com[36]

Not necessarily. In *A Perfect Mess: The Hidden Benefits of Disorder*, David Freedman and Eric Abrahamson argue that messiness is actually a strength and should be "celebrated rather than avoided." They provide evidence that there are significant benefits to disorder. Andy Rooney, the quirky commentator for *60 Minutes*, agreed

---

36. https://onsizzle.com/i/s-of-leaving-your-sh-t-all-over-the-life-changing-magic-1847011

saying, "Creativity doesn't come out of order; it comes out of messiness."

For example, Alexander Fleming discovered penicillin while sorting through his cluttered lab after returning from a long vacation. If his lab had been clean and organized, we might not have access to life saving antibiotics. Albert Einstein, probably one of the most creative minds of the 20th century, challenged the enemies of clutter by asking, "If a cluttered desk is a sign of a cluttered mind, then what is an empty desk a sign of?"

Rough diamonds may sometimes be mistaken for worthless pebbles.
- Sir Thomas Browne

DISTRACTION

The founder of JetBlue, David Neeleman, has said that if there were a pill that cured ADD, he wouldn't take it. As Matt Curry explains in *The ADD Entrepreneur*, "Your flaw may actually be your superpower. I've never viewed ADD as a negative. Instead, I've embraced it." Cameron Herold, the former COO of 1-800-GOT-JUNK?, agrees. "ADD doesn't have to be a problem at all. It's one of the key things that makes us successful as an entrepreneur... ADD allows us to see all the things related to our business that others miss.... ADD is actually a strength."

Edward Hallowell is the author of *Driven to Distraction* and one of the leading experts on ADD. His research confirms this positive perspective of ADD. He created a table of "mirror traits" that describes both the weaknesses and the corresponding strengths of ADD. This is one more example of the connection between flaws and awesome.

Positive	Negative
Curious	Distractible
Creative	Impulsive
Energetic	Hyperactive, Restless
Eager	Intrusive
Sees connections others miss	Can't stay on point
Totally involved in what he/she is doing	Forgetful
Spontaneous	Disorganized
Persistent	Stubborn
Flashes of brilliance	Inconsistent
Sensitive	Moody

DYSLEXIA

Paul grew up in a hard-working, middle-class family in Southern California. In second grade, he still didn't know the alphabet. Efforts by his teachers, parents, and siblings didn't seem to help. He was eventually diagnosed with both dyslexia and ADHD. After failing a few grades and being expelled from several schools, he finally graduated from high school with a 1.2 grade point average and a ranking of 1,482 out of 1,500 students.

Based on his disability and poor performance in school, most people wouldn't have predicted success for Paul. In fact, Paul himself was often concerned that he would end up homeless. He started a small business selling school supplies and copies in a store so small that he had to move the copier out to the sidewalk. The business eventually grew to 1200 locations in ten different countries and, in 2004, Paul Orfalea sold Kinko's to FedEx for more than $2 billion.

How did a dyslexic guy who can't read or write build such a successful business? Orfalea argues that he succeeded because of his disability, not in spite of it. Because of his weaknesses, he had to trust others and rely on them to help him run the business. For example, he needed people to assist him with correspondence. This evolved into a culture of teamwork and collaboration that separated Kinko's from their competitors. Paul hired people who were strong where he was weak.

Because he was restless, he spent most of his time out of his office and in the stores, observing the practices of frontline employees. Because he was impulsive, he quickly implemented new ideas throughout the organization. His intuitive intelligence and racing mind made him impatient and easily frustrated, but many employees credit these traits with creating a sense of urgency that motivated people to make changes and improvements.

Orfalea wrote *Copy This! Lessons from a Hyperactive Dyslexic Who Turned a Bright Idea into One of America's Best Companies* with journalist Ann Marsh, but because of his dyslexia, he's never been able to read his own book. In it, he credits his disabilities for his success and says he thinks everyone should have dyslexia and ADHD. During his many speaking engagements, he advises audiences to "like yourself, not despite your flaws and so-called deficits, but because of them."

Paul Orfalea didn't just appreciate his own weaknesses; he also created an organization that appreciated the weaknesses of its employees. He turned Kinko's into a pink goldfish by demonstrating sensitivity for the limitations of others, such as stubbornness, impatience, disorganization, and impulsiveness. Since he wasn't perfect, he didn't expect perfection from others. He readily admitted his own flaws and accepted the flaws of his employees. Because he couldn't do everything well and relied on others to complete essential tasks, he also allowed others to find team members that complemented their weaknesses.

Additionally, he wasn't afraid to be different, and he encouraged his employees to approach their work in unique and creative ways. This created a culture of innovation, trust, and teamwork that made Kinko's a perennial favorite on Fortune's 100 Best Companies to Work For.

It's okay to be disorganized. It's okay to be distracted. It's okay to be dyslexic. It's not just okay. It's fantastic. These are just three of the flaws that can make you awesome.

Instead of trying to create perfect organizations, we need to appreciate our company's limitations and make sure that we don't let what we cannot do interfere with what we can do. Then we need to go even farther. If we really appreciated our company's weaknesses, we would amplify them instead of trying to fix them. We would exaggerate our apparent flaws.

CHAPTER 15

AMPLIFY

*"If everything seems under control,
you're not going fast enough."*

– Mario Andretti

Amplifying is the essence of flaunting your weakness and weirdness. This is the act of not only shining a light on what makes you unique but actually turning up the dial on your weirdness or weakness.

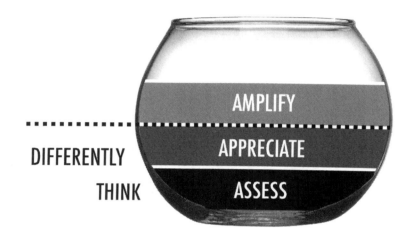

To steal a phrase from the rockumentary *This is Spinal Tap*, you lean in and "turn it up to 11." In the movie, lead guitarist Nigel Tufnel, played by Christopher Guest, proudly demonstrates an amplifier whose knobs are marked from zero to eleven, instead of the usual zero to ten.

Photo Credit: Wikipedia Commons[37]

37. https://en.wikipedia.org/wiki/Up_to_eleven

In 2002, the phrase was entered into the *Shorter Oxford English Dictionary* with the definition[38] "up to maximum volume." Here is the dialogue from the movie between Nigel and Marty DiBergi, the Director, played by Rob Reiner:

> **Nigel:** See. The numbers all go to eleven. Look, right across the board, eleven, eleven, eleven and...
>
> **Marty:** Oh, I see. And most amps go up to ten?
>
> **Nigel:** Exactly.
>
> **Marty:** Does that mean it's louder? Is it any louder?
>
> **Nigel:** Well, it's one louder, isn't it? It's not ten. You see, most blokes, you know, will be playing at ten. You're on ten here, all the way up, all the way up, all the way up, you're on ten on your guitar. Where can you go from there? Where?
>
> **Marty:** I don't know.
>
> **Nigel:** Nowhere. Exactly. What we do is, if we need that extra push over the cliff, you know what we do?
>
> **Marty:** Put it up to eleven.
>
> **Nigel:** Eleven. Exactly. One louder.
>
> **Marty:** Why don't you just make ten louder and make ten be the top number and make that a little louder? [Long Pause.]
>
> **Nigel:** These go to eleven.

---

38. https://en.wikipedia.org/wiki/Up_to_eleven

Amplifying isn't just awareness, knowing your strengths and weaknesses. It isn't just appreciation, valuing your strengths and weaknesses. Amplifying is getting weirder by getting weaker. Amplifying is going even farther. For some, you've gone too far. For others, you haven't gone far enough.

There are two parts to amplifying: maximizing and minimizing.

- Maximizing is spending MORE time, energy, and resources on what makes us weird and weak.

- Minimizing is spending LESS time, energy, and resources conforming to traditional models of success.

MAXIMIZE

Look back at your assessment results from the previous chapter. What are your organization's unique weaknesses? What if you maximized them? We're going to challenge you to take it "one louder." Here are 11 sample questions and answers that might help.

1. Are your products cheap? Make them cheaper.

Some customers want the most inexpensive option, regardless of quality.

2. Are your services too expensive? Increase the price.

Some customers will see them as luxurious, lavish, or extravagant.

3. Is your company boring? Make it even more dull.

Some customers like to keep things simple or prefer a conservative approach.

4. Are your products too complex? Make them even more confusing.

Some customers will see them as intricate, sophisticated, and challenging.

5. Is your service too impersonal? Remove people altogether.

Some customers prefer automated systems.

6. Is your company too serious? Become even more serious.

Some customers will see you as professional, business-like, and distinguished.

7. Is your company too silly? Become even more ridiculous.

Some customers will see you as irreverent and hilarious.

8. Are your products too offensive? Make them even more shocking.

Some customers want stuff that is bold and daring.

9. Do you offer slow service? What if you made it even slower?

Some customers enjoy the sense of anticipation.

10. Are you failing to offer enough options? What if you offered even fewer?

Some customers get overwhelmed with too many choices.

11. Are you too cynical? What if you got even more pessimistic?

Some customers will see it as realistic or satirical.

The defeatists at Despair.com have turned negativity into a business by creating demotivational posters that parody the inspirational messages decorating corporate conference rooms across the country. Here are ten of our favorites.

QUALITY – The race for quality has no finish line—so technically, it's more like a death march.

TEAMWORK – A few harmless flakes working together can unleash an avalanche of destruction.

TEAMS – Together, we can do the work of one.

SYNERGY – A code word lazy people use when they want you to do all the work.

CUSTOMER CARE – If we really cared for the customer, we'd send them somewhere better.

CUSTOMER DISSERVICE – Because we're not satisfied until you're not satisfied.

APATHY – If we don't take care of the customer, maybe they'll stop bugging us.

MOTIVATION – If a pretty poster and a cute saying are all it takes to motivate you, you probably have a very easy job. The kind robots will be doing soon.

It might sound ridiculous to amplify your organization's weaknesses. In fact, this is exactly the opposite (remember the chapter on Opposing) of what most companies do. The traditional approach

DESPAIR

IT'S ALWAYS DARKEST JUST BEFORE IT GOES PITCH BLACK.

involves highlighting positive features and repairing or obscuring any negative ones.

For example, the message on a bag of Domino sugar explains that "sugar is a 100% natural simple carbohydrate. Carbohydrates are an important part of any balanced diet. Sugar contains no fat or cholesterol and has 15 calories per teaspoon." They make it sound like the perfect food.

Domino's strategy seems to make sense. Why would you want to tell potential customers about what's wrong with your stuff? It seems ridiculous. And that is why very few companies do it.

However, there's a major problem with this approach. We all know that sugar isn't the perfect food and that undermines our ability to trust Domino. They aren't being honest.

We know that nothing is perfect. Pretending that your stuff is flawless hurts your brand. In contrast, acknowledging that your stuff isn't perfect makes it easier to love your brand.

According to Chip and Dan Heath, authors of *Made to Stick*, openly admitting limitations helps us build trust. This is true when discussing our own limitations or those of our ideas, products, or services. "We've all come across salespeople who are reluctant to admit any weakness in their product or service, no matter how insignificant. As many a sales guru has pointed out, building trust involves being candid, and being candid involves admitting that your products aren't flawless. Admitting weakness can, oddly enough, make your core ideas more powerful." Similarly, brand consultant Vicki Stirling believes that "admitting mistakes and flaws are actually really good tools to encourage loyalty."

And to be clear, this isn't about admitting, and then apologizing for, your product's weaknesses. Remember, flaunt means "to parade without shame." Weaknesses aren't shameful. They are something to celebrate.

So, another way to amplify is to brag, or at least be honest, about your weakness and uniqueness. Make sure everyone knows what is wrong with you.

Remember Alamo Drafthouse. They turned a customer complaint into an advertisement. They didn't try to hide their weaknesses. They turned on the spotlight.

Another example is Jimmy Vee at Gravitational Marketing. He calls himself "The Five-Foot High Marketing Guy." He doesn't try to hide his short stature. He celebrates it, which makes him likable, memorable, and interesting.

Maximizing is about spending MORE time, energy, and resources on what makes us weird and weak. Now let's focus on minimizing, which is about spending LESS time, energy, and resources conforming to traditional models of success.

MINIMIZE

As a transplant to the South from the Midwest, David enjoys the many new types of foliage. After several years, he is still amazed to see flowers bloom on bushes in early January. One very popular southern tree is the Crepe Myrtle. It caught his attention because of the way it is pruned. In the winter, you can see rows and rows of trees that have been cut back severely with only the largest branches remaining. This annual pruning maintains the health and appearance of the tree.

In our efforts to make our companies well-rounded and multi-faceted, we often develop branches that are unproductive. Unfortunately, we don't prune them and they end up sapping our strength.

Every company has a limited amount of time, energy, and resources. Minimizing (pruning) allows us to conserve those resources and use them in ways that improve our effectiveness.

> *To fulfill some commitments, others must be excluded.*
> - *Chris Guillebeau,* The Art of Non-Conformity

Minimizing is unconventional, but it is a strategy with many advocates. Marcus Buckingham, author of *The One Thing You Need to Know*, argues that the most important thing to know about personal success is "if you don't like it, stop doing it." Peter Drucker, the father of modern management, encouraged companies to practice "organized abandonment." In *The Art of Non-Conformity,* Guillebeau refers to it as "radical exclusion."

Leadership guru Tom Peters recommends that you go a step further and get a "stop counselor" for your strategic planning meetings to help you eliminate unnecessary or distracting goals and activities. Jim Collins, author of *Good to Great,* argues that both business and individuals should create a stop-doing list. Here are a few tips from his website:

• Start an actual, physical list of things to stop doing.

• When you add a new activity to your to-do list, select an activity to stop doing.

• Rank your activities from most to least important. Drop the bottom 20%.

• Don't devote resources to activities that don't pass the preceding tests.

This is difficult advice because we're taught to be strong in all areas in order to succeed. Organizations experience intense pressure to moderate their unique characteristics instead of maximizing or minimizing them. Conventional wisdom says that our organizations should strive for perfection and balance. However, this isn't true. In fact, in order to be the best in one area, brands have to be willing to be the worst (or at least poor) in others.

For example, the two teams in the 2010 Super Bowl were the Indianapolis Colts and the New Orleans Saints. The Colts had the worst running game of any team in the NFL and the Saints had one of the worst defenses. However, the Colts also had one of the best passing offenses and the Saints made up for their poor defense with a league-leading offense. Both teams were the best in one area and the worst in another.

In 2013, the Seattle Seahawks won the Super Bowl. That same year, they were the most penalized team in the league.

Matthias Schlitte offers an even more interesting example of this principle. He began practicing arm-wrestling when he was 16 years old but has only been training the muscles in his right arm. When you see a picture of him, it looks like he has some sort of genetic deformity and he does. It's called KTS, which causes one of a person's four limbs to grow much larger than the others.

His right forearm is nearly 18 inches around, but his left forearm measures just 6 inches. It seems like the only muscles that he has are in his right arm. This is a huge advantage in arm wrestling because his opponents are determined by weight class. People wrestle against others of similar weight.

Photo Credit: Wikimedia Commons

Matthias' wrestling arm is much larger than that of his competitors because they have bodies with normal proportions. Unfortunately, this means that much of their weight is in parts of their bodies that don't help them with arm wrestling.

Schlitte can spend additional time and energy exercising his right arm (maximizing) because he doesn't have to bother with building the rest of his body (minimizing). He is weak in many areas so that he can be incredibly strong in the area that is the most important. This makes him unbalanced, but it also makes him successful.

Google is a great organizational example of minimizing. Yahoo was the search engine leader before Google became the dominant force that it is today. So how did Google win? There are a lot of answers to that question, but one is particularly useful for our purposes.

Look at Yahoo!'s homepage. The first thing you probably notice is how full it is. There are innumerable links, stories, and banners. There's news, weather, sports, and more. Everything you need, and a lot you probably don't need, is right there.

Now, look at Google's homepage. The first thing you notice is how empty it is. There is just a search box. Nothing you need is right there, so you'll have to search for it.

Google didn't try to beat Yahoo! by finding a way to put even more information, links, and advertisements on their homepage. Instead, Google practiced minimizing. They did less, not more.

Google's approach framed all of Yahoo!'s strengths as weaknesses. Yahoo! wasn't informative. It was cluttered. Yahoo! wasn't helpful. It was confusing. Yahoo! was controlling. They told you what to read instead of helping you find what you wanted.

In contrast, Google wasn't cluttered. It was clean and neat. Google wasn't confusing. It was simple. Google wasn't telling you where to go. It was there to help you find what you wanted.

Google dramatically underperformed (minimized) compared to Yahoo!'s ability to put everything in one place, but this allowed them to over-deliver (maximize) on what many customers wanted, which was faster and more relevant search.

We hope that by now you're ready to turn up the volume on your organization's weaknesses. Amplifying is essential, but it doesn't work without alignment. You can't turn up the volume success-fully unless someone wants it louder. The final step in creating a pink goldfish is to match your brand's unique flaws with the right people, products, positioning, and places.

CHAPTER 16

ALIGN

*"Every individual has a place to fill in the world
and is important in some respect,
whether he chooses to be so or not."*
- Nathaniel Hawthorne

Most of this book has been about being different; this final section is about similarity. It's time to find people who are weird like you, who have the same weaknesses, and who like your style. It's time to move to places where your flaws fit in and where your products are perfect. Aligning is matching, connecting, and linking your organization's uniqueness with the people, both internally and externally, who value that distinctiveness.

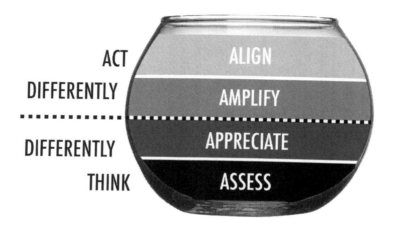

Let's start with your organization's people. If any of this is going to work, your company needs the right personnel. An unconventional brand strategy requires unconventional staff to execute that strategy. If flaws make your brand awesome, then maybe flaws make your people awesome. Are you looking for weird workers, strange staff, eccentric employees, and abnormal associates?

"Find the freaks! Sign 'em up! Make 'em your partners!
Let 'em help you make a revolution!"
– Tom Peters

PEOPLE

Since weaknesses are important clues to employees' strengths, we need to start by identifying employees' strengths and weaknesses before they even begin working for us. This assessment is also important for our existing employees. We should assess our teams, work groups, departments, and divisions in order to understand our people better and help them understand each other.

Publix Supermarkets has been on the list of Best Companies to Work For in America by *Fortune* for over 25 years. They believe it is possible to measure a job candidate's natural tendency to provide great service. Their hiring decisions are based on a person's strengths and their fit with the company's culture.

Effective management is not about changing people. It is about accepting and respecting who they are and finding ways to help them succeed.

Saddleback Church, located in Lake Forest, California, is the eighth-largest church in America. Their pastor, Rick Warren, is the author of *The Purpose Driven Life*, which has sold more than 25 million copies. Warren believes that "the secret of achieving results is to focus on your strengths, and the strengths of those you work with, rather than focusing on weaknesses." He manages his organization and his employees and volunteers with this philosophy.

He argues that "great organizations position people for success rather than trying to eliminate all their weaknesses.... When an employee fails because he doesn't have the strengths to match the job, the fault is management's, not the employee's.... In order to use the strengths of people we must be willing to put up with their weaknesses."

As managers, we need to identify the unique value that each employee can contribute. This should be part of the evaluation process. Instead of trying to find and fix weaknesses, we can focus on the person's strengths and look for ways to deploy those strengths at work.

Ann Taylor, a women's clothing retailer, helps managers to understand that their employees' weaknesses are linked to their strengths. Because of this perspective, managers don't try to fix their employees' flaws. Instead, they find partners within the organization that complement the employee's weaknesses. Managers also attempt to adapt their own approach to accommodate the employee's unique style.

For example, Claudia was very analytical and intense. She had a strong need to know as much information as possible about issues that affected her work. When she didn't get information in a timely manner, she got frustrated and this created tension between her and her manager. It also created problems within the entire work team.

"An average manager might have identified this behavior as a weakness and lectured Claudia on how to control her need for information. Judi, however, realized that this weakness'was an aspect of Claudia's greatest strength: her analytical mind. Claudia would never be able to rein it in, at least not for long."

Instead of trying to fix Claudia's weakness, her manager made an effort to dramatically increase the amount of information that she shared with Claudia. They scheduled regular meetings and daily phone calls. This allowed Claudia to focus more time and energy on her strengths, which improved her performance.

We need to encourage and develop each individual's unique abilities. Great managers help people to become more of who they are. One way to do this is to train strengths. Too often, our training efforts are focused on remediating weaknesses. A more effective approach is to help employees amplify their existing strengths through books, seminars, and coaching.

We also need to stop cross-training and focus on specialization instead. People aren't machines and their skills and interests are not necessarily interchangeable. Best Buy's employees are geeks that know a lot about a narrow range of products. A mobile phone expert won't necessarily be an expert in car stereo installation. How could you help your people learn even more about their current job responsibilities?

Patagonia hires "dirtbags." Instead of looking for employees with business skills or sales experience, Patagonia selects people who have a natural passion for the outdoors. This is something that cannot be taught in a training program. Dirtbags have many weaknesses, but these are less important than their strengths.

W.L. Gore & Associates has been on the list of Best Companies to Work For in America for 25 years. Their employees do not have traditional job descriptions. They are allowed to add new responsibilities that match their strengths (alignment) and can decline those that don't (avoidance). Instead of following development plans developed by their supervisors, Gore employees create their own customized personal growth plans.

Instead of forcing people to fit in, we need to help them find the right fit. We need to help employees discover activities and responsibilities that match their unique characteristics.

We need to identify the strength/weakness combinations that match the needs of our team and clearly understand what tradeoffs we are comfortable making. We won't have to adapt as much if we find people who fit the requirements of the job.

Unfortunately, most companies spend far more money on training people to fit in than they do on selecting people for a particular job. Once we find the right people for the job, we'll need to work continually with our employees to help them identify and create responsibilities that match their unique characteristics.

One way to maximize alignment is to let people choose their work. 3M and Google know this. That is why they allow their employees to work on projects they are passionate about during the work week. Atlassian, an Australian software company regularly allows all of their employees to take 24 consecutive hours to develop their own innovative product or service ideas. RedHat, Wikipedia, and Apache run almost exclusively on the efforts of willing volunteers.

Lest this seem like some kind of touchy-feely employee-centric nonsense, another important action step is to fire faster. In the words of Marcus Buckingham, "Never stop caring for your people. You will rarely fire a person too early. Tough love is built on love." We waste far too much time trying to turn people into the person that we need. If an employee doesn't fit, we shouldn't try to make them fit. We should set them free.

SAS assesses and categorizes clinical programmers based on their strengths and weaknesses. The four profiles are: Scientist, Statistician, Developer, and Lead Programmer. Managers are trained to assign tasks to programmers based on their strengths instead of trying to fix their weaknesses. SAS believes that employees will be more motivated and perform at a higher level when they are allowed to focus on activities that fit their strengths and avoid those that rely on their weaknesses.

At SAS, managers are given scenarios with specific projects to be completed by certain people. They are then asked to choose the right person for each task. They are taught to consider what each person likes to do and does well in addition to what the person doesn't like to do and does poorly. "Assigning projects might be the most critical aspect of allowing programmers to exercise their full motivation. Give a highly motivated programmer a job that he/she does not see as important or is not good at, and you will undoubtedly see his/her motivation decrease sharply."

SAS differentiates different types of work and identifies which will be best assigned to each profile. Lead Programmers, for instance, are charged with project organization. Scientists are charged with documenting the details of programming. Developers spend most of their time actually developing. And Statisticians focus on how the programming compares to statistical models. The whole idea is to let Developers be Developers and Scientists be Scientists without everyone needing to be everything.

If we want people to be the best, we need to let them be the worst. It isn't possible to be the best at everything. If we are helping employees do more work that matches their strengths, then we also need to allow employees to stop doing work that puts a spotlight on their weaknesses.

Instead of trying to change a person to fit a particular position, transfer them. Help them find the right match between who they are and what they do. This option is especially feasible in large corporations where there is a wide variety of positions.

Instead of rehabilitating a difficult employee, try redirecting them instead. It can be easier to change a job than to change a person. It is often possible to make a slight change in job responsibilities (alignment) and see a large improvement in performance. It isn't enough to simply get the right people in the right seats, as Jim Collins suggests in *Good to Great*. We sometimes need to redesign the seats and the seating arrangements on the bus.

Could we assign them more of the work that they do well? Can we eliminate aspects of the work that they do poorly? Remember the pruning example from the last chapter. Eliminating the unproductive aspects of the person's job can give them more time and energy to invest in the areas where they are productive.

Stryker, a large surgical equipment company, has documented significant financial gains from allowing employees to avoid activities that draw on their weaknesses. In one example, they saved over $1 million by moving an employee from a role as an individual performer, where he struggled, into a supervisory position, where he thrived. His new role also changed his level of engagement at work. His supervisors felt his attitude as well as performance had critically improved.

Another employee struggled with paperwork but excelled in sales. The employee's performance improved significantly once he was no longer required to complete paperwork. His managers at Stryker eliminated the problem by redistributing it among team members who could more comfortably balance it with their engineering contributions.

Effective managers create teams with complementary strengths and weaknesses. Although no single employee is going to be perfectly balanced and well-rounded, we need to build work groups and departments that include employees whose strengths and weaknesses complement those of their co-workers.

We're too busy trying to make everyone the same. We use cross-training and other methods to make everyone capable of doing any job at any time, or we assemble homogenous teams of people with the same strengths and the same weaknesses.

Very few employees are completely effective on their own but they can be a valuable part of a team. We need to find team members with complementary skills and help them work together to accomplish the work that needs to be done. By combining people instead of fixing people, we can improve the performance of each individual and the entire team.

Teamwork doesn't mean that everybody does the same thing. It means that everyone contributes what they do best.

David met Kelly when she was an undergraduate student in his management class. She was a great salesperson. Selling seemed like the ideal fit for her skills and personality. She was a natural.

She was so good at her job that she sold insurance to David during the class. She didn't wait for a break. When David was complaining about the lack of service from his current insurance agent, she raised her hand and suggested that he switch to her agency. David filled out the forms the next week and was a customer before the course was over.

Kelly sounds like the perfect employee but she had a problem. She was incredibly disorganized and was inefficient with the essential administrative tasks that her job required. She frequently lost important forms, which created major inconveniences for her clients and caused costly delays within her agency. Her office was littered with piles of papers, discarded fast food containers, dirty dishes, and boxes overflowing with marketing materials. This is a classic problem with salespeople. She was terrible at paperwork but wonderful with people work.

Kelly's manager realized that Kelly's talent for sales was a rare and valuable gift. Instead of criticizing Kelly for poor performance or sending her to training, Kelly's boss simply hired a person to handle the paperwork and create an organized work environment for Kelly. This freed Kelly to do more of what she did so well and made her much happier and more fulfilled in her work. In return, Kelly's boss got increased sales and revenue.

As managers, we are employees so the pink goldfish principles also apply to us. It isn't enough to help our employees flaunt their weaknesses. As managers, we have to embrace our flaws as well.

We fail when we try to please everyone by becoming perfect, by fixing all our weaknesses. We fail when we believe it is possible for everyone to like us, respect us, and appreciate us.

Our employees are all too aware of our apparent weaknesses and wish that we could overcome them to become a more effective manager. It can be tempting to try to become a perfect and well-rounded leader, but this is not an effective strategy. Instead, we should acknowledge that we cannot please everyone, hire employees that are strong where we are weak, look for activities that fit our unique style, and admit our flaws to our employees.

When assessing potential job candidates, it is important to consider more than just the job responsibilities. We should also consider their fit with our management style. For example, if we want employees who take initiative, then we shouldn't hire folks who require a lot of direction.

We should seek out people who complement specific weaknesses that we have. Additionally, we need mentors and organizational allies who will help us create an environment that highlights our strengths and minimizes our weaknesses.

We can't please everyone but we can help them understand and accept our apparent weaknesses. It's important to be honest with our employees, managers, and co-workers about our strengths and weaknesses. This will help foster honesty about their strengths and weaknesses as well.

One way to do this is to write a "how to deal with me" memo. Marshall Goldsmith suggests this approach in his book, *What Got You Here Won't Get You There*. Even though Goldsmith's job is to help successful executives overcome their interpersonal quirks to become even more effective, he admits that this isn't always possible. Because of this reality, he encourages his clients to write a memo to their employees that outlines their unique qualities and explains how to effectively deal with their personal and managerial idiosyncrasies. This advice is supported by persuasion research which indicates that admitting weaknesses makes our ideas more powerful.

George is a manager at a small magazine publisher, but he doesn't like to accompany his clients, mainly vendors and advertisers, to the endless formal events in his industry. He finds many of the people boring and has a difficult time engaging them in conversation. So he doesn't go. He told his employees that these banquets drain him of his energy and that he doesn't perform well in those situations.

In contrast, Brad, one of George's employees, truly enjoys getting dressed up and interacting with advertising clients at formal gatherings. Because of this, George now delegates these activities to Brad. This allows George to focus on other areas in which he is more interested and more skilled. It also allows Brad to grow in his career and to build relationships with key players in the publishing industry.

> *I think normality is whatever the majority decides it will be,*
> *and in our company people with autism are the norm.*
> *– Thorkil Sonne, CEO of Specialisterne*

Thorkil Sonne is the founder of Specialisterne, a Danish software-testing company. He started the company because his son has autism and Sonne wanted him to have a meaningful job. Nearly 75% of the company's employees have some form of autism, but Sonne doesn't hire them because he's trying to be charitable. He hires them because their disability is the perfect fit for the work his company does.

Sonne explains that his "ambition was to use the autism characteristics as a competitive advantage." His company's work matches the unique skill sets of people with autism spectrum disorders with a major need in the field of software and game testing. Characteristics of autism include intense focus, high tolerance for repetition, and a strong memory. These are the same skills that are necessary to be effective as a software tester.

When people with autism work at Specialisterne, they're not disabled; they're uniquely qualified. SAP, the global software giant, was so impressed with Specialisterne's success that they are now looking for hundreds of people with autism to work as software testers.

Similarly, MindSpark is also hiring people with autism as software testers. They currently have 30 employees and their goal is to grow to more than 100 over the next two years.

MindSpark's clients include many high-profile brands and Fortune 500 companies such as Fox Networks Group. Ben Hope, CIO for Fox Networks Group, explained that "their team has exceeded our initial expectations. In addition to a very beneficial value proposition—providing us with reasonably priced resources in the same time zone as our development teams—our internal team has thoroughly enjoyed the win-win feeling of this particular business model."

Another example is Auticon, a London-based IT firm. They only hire individuals with autism. While many of their employees have had a hard time finding employment, Auticon views what most employers see as weakness as an opportunity.

PRODUCTS AND POSITIONING

Amplification is only effective if you discover customers who want more of what you do well and who don't care about what you don't do well.

Remember Alt Hotels from the Chapter 6 on Flaunting? Their ads focus on what they don't do. They are attracting the customer who wants what they have and repelling the customers who want what they don't have. This is crucial. According to Frei and Morriss in *Uncommon Service*, "Excellence requires underperforming on the things your customers value least, so you can over-deliver on the dimensions they value most."

IKEA is a great example. They underperform AND over-deliver. Most furniture stores have salespeople who help you choose high-quality, expensive furniture that will last for a very long time. You might be able to pass it along to your children. Once you commit to the purchase, your selections will be delivered to your home and assembled for you.

IKEA is purposely not like the ordinary furniture store. Compared to traditional furniture stores, Ikea underperforms. They have a lot of weaknesses. They don't have salespeople, and it's hard to find what you need as you wander through their gigantic warehouse. They don't have high-quality furniture. It isn't expensive. It won't last for generations. They won't deliver it. You have to assemble it.

It's easy to see how IKEA underperforms, but it's hard to see how they over-deliver. This is crucial. They discovered that many customers saw traditional furniture store's strengths as weaknesses and that those same customers saw IKEA's weaknesses as strengths.

For example, salespeople can be helpful but they can also make customers feel uncomfortable and pressured. Ikea doesn't pressure you.

Purchasing lifetime furniture is expensive and a big commitment. Ikea furniture is inexpensive and it isn't a big commitment. You can just replace it when it goes out of style or breaks.

Furniture delivery takes days and sometimes weeks. Furniture from Ikea goes home with you today.

Traditional furniture is assembled for you. When you assemble your Ikea furniture, even though the process is frustrating, you have a sense of accomplishment from being involved in the process.

IKEA discovered what customers value most and then over-delivered in those areas. They also discovered what customers valued least and underperformed in those areas.

If brands want to attract the right customers and repel the wrong customers, they need to spend significant time answering these four questions.

1. Which customers love you?

2. How can you create even deeper connections with them?

3. Which customers hate you?

4. How can you make them even more unhappy?

PLACES

If you want to find weird employees and weird customers for your weird products, you might need to go to a weird place.

One place that is famous for being weird is Austin, the capital of Texas. They are known around the world for their "Keep Austin Weird" campaign, which has defined the city for decades. But it's fair to ask a simple question. Does weird work? Absolutely. Let's look at the facts.

With a population of just under one million residents, Austin is the 11th biggest U.S. city. They have been rated as the best city in the U.S. for jobs. They also have been the third fastest growing U.S. city. They've been recognized as the best city for growing businesses, and Austin was one of the top three travel hotspots in 2014.

But maybe it's easier to be weird when you're a big city and a state capital. What about a smaller city like Portland, Oregon, population 650,000? They've adopted the slogan "Keep Portland Weird." How are they doing?

Portland is also doing very well. They were ranked one of the top ten best places to retire in the U.S. They are the second greenest city in the entire world. They are the most bike-friendly city in the U.S. and the second most liked city in the U.S.

But even though Portland is smaller than Austin, it isn't really a small city. Asheville, North Carolina, has a population of under 100,000, and they are trying to stay weird too. They like to say that "If you're too weird for Asheville, you're too weird."

Deanna Loew, an Asheville resident, proudly proclaims that Asheville is the strangest place you will ever visit and has the weirdest people in the country.

"Asheville has an eclectic mix of hippies, doctors, and southerners. We are smack dab in the middle of the Bible Belt, the Blue Ridge Parkway, and one of the biggest medical centers in the U.S. I consistently see a man with a purple mohawk hula-hooping in the middle of Pack Square in a tutu. When you go to the local grocery store, you are confronted with hippies, suburban housewives, doctors in scrubs, real life cowboys, and a vast array of other eclectic Ashevillians. I truly do not think that there will ever be a city more diverse than Asheville. We may be weird, but those who live in Asheville love this quirky little town. Yes, we are strange. Yes, we are proud. Yes, we are Asheville."

And weird is working. Asheville has been named the new freak capital of the U.S. They are one of the top ten places in the U.S. to reinvent your life and one of the top ten most beautiful places in the U.S. They are also one of the top 25 best places for businesses and careers in the country.

Weird works in America, but it also works globally. In 2014, Samari, Yamartino, and Davari compiled statistics on every country in the world to discover what each country was best at. Here are some of the highlights. This may help as you search for a place that wants what your brand creates.

Canada leads the world in maple syrup and asteroid impacts. If you're trying to sell artificial pancake syrup, you probably shouldn't do it in Canada. But if you're selling equipment for doomsday preppers, you might find a receptive market.

Australia is the leader in deadly animals and melanoma. There are a lot of ways to die in Australia. This might be a great market for sunscreen, health care services, or anxiety medication.

China is the highest in CO_2 emissions and renewable energy. They are working both sides of that equation, creating and solving the pollution problem. If you provide emissions control systems, China is a potential customer. If you are in the renewable energy industry, China is a potential partner.

Greenland provides the most personal space. That's a positive way to say that no one lives there. It isn't a big market, but what do they do with all that space? Maybe you can sell them a fence or an ATV or some cows.

Russia offers the most raspberries and nuclear warheads. There seem to be opportunities here for organic farmers, agri-tainers, and global arms dealers.

Netherlands has the tallest people on earth. If your brand specializes in weird sizes, the Dutch need your help.

New Zealand is the best at rugby and sheep.

The U.S. has the most lawnmower deaths and Nobel laureates. Apparently, we have both the dumbest and smartest people on earth. Maybe you need to start researching some lawnmower safety innovations or better ways to cut the grass. You might be able to get some sheep from New Zealand.

There's an illusion that there is a perfect place with perfect customers and perfect employees. There is no such thing as a perfect place.

For example, David moved from Wisconsin in the Midwest to North Carolina in the South. The weather is much warmer in North Carolina, and the winters are much milder than in Wisconsin. But it isn't perfect.

Wisconsin has harsh winters featuring extreme cold and blizzards, but it doesn't have hurricanes. However, Wisconsin does have tornadoes. If you try to avoid tornadoes and hurricanes, you'll likely end up in a place that has floods.

Southern California is known for its consistently warm temperatures, but it's also plagued by drought, mudslides, wildfires, and earthquakes. Colorado has beautiful mountains, but it also has avalanches, something you don't have to worry about in Kansas.

There's plenty of sunshine and warm temperatures in Phoenix, but it also has dust storms.

Vancouver in British Columbia is a great illustration of how the weaknesses and strengths of a place are connected.

On the positive side, Vancouver

- is one of the most livable cities in the world.

- has the fourth highest quality of living on earth.

- is the tenth cleanest city on earth.

- has the fourth thinnest residents in Canada.

On the negative side, Vancouver also

- has the worst traffic congestion in Canada.

- has the second most unaffordable housing on earth.

- has one of the highest crime rates in North America.

- is the most densely populated Canadian city.

It's easy to see how some of the city's weaknesses are directly related to its strengths. Traffic congestion and unaffordable housing are due to the area's quality of life. Everyone wants to live there.

Vancouver's dense population is both a positive and negative. For sustainability experts and city planners, density is one measure of a city's success. However, if you're from Greenland and you're looking for some personal space, you're not going to find it in Vancouver.

As you build your pink goldfish, you need awareness, appreciation, amplification, and alignment. You need to match your weirdness and weakness with the right people, products, positioning, and places.

SECTION IV

CLOSING

CHAPTER 17

TOP FIVE TAKEAWAYS

"Don't try to stand out from the crowd.
Avoid crowds altogether."

- Hugh MacLeod

HERE ARE THE TOP FIVE TAKEAWAYS FROM PINK GOLDFISH:

1. WEIRD WORKS

It's easy to follow the crowd. It's easy to blend in. It seems smart to do what other brands are doing. It feels safe. But it's not. Successful brands stick out. They are different. They are unusual.

2. THERE ARE MANY DIFFERENT WAYS TO BE DIFFERENT

We provided a lot of examples in this book, but we don't recommend that you imitate those examples. We want you to see that there is an infinite number of ways to be unique. You can learn the principle from other brands, but you have to practice it in your own way. Who can you antagonize? How can you do the opposite? What can you withhold?

3. BE UNAPOLOGETIC

Be proud of what your brand does and what it doesn't do. Be proud of your brand's strengths and weaknesses. Don't apologize for your flaws and don't try to fix them. Instead, exploit your brand's imperfections.

4. TO PLEASE SOME CUSTOMERS, YOU HAVE TO DISPLEASE OTHERS

You can't be good at everything. You can't make everyone happy. So don't try. In fact, we think you should go out of your way to make some people unhappy. Choose whom you will reject. Decide whom to repel. Do it deliberately.

5. START SMALL—START NOW

You don't have to change your entire strategy all at once. You don't have to turn around completely, just swerve to the left or right. Look for a way to be micro-weird. Little things have a big impact (remember lagniappe). Don't wait. Deviate.

Here's how you can help us create more pink goldfish:

- apply what you've learned in this book to your brand

- share the book with others

- bring us in to speak at your conference

- book us for a workshop or strategy session

- connect with us on LinkedIn

ABOUT THE AUTHORS

WEIRD THINGS ABOUT STAN:

First thing he does when visiting a new country is to eat at McDonald's.

Favorite McDonald's was in India because he got to order a McTikka.

Stan is not related to Michael Phelps, but he has webbed toes and is banned from Olympic swimming.

Is obsessed with acronyms and bar tricks.

Has never broken a bone.

Have two sons and male cat. My wife is the sole female in the house.

Met my wife at baggage claim in the Amsterdam airport.

Is infamous for doing a weird flaming shot called the "Statue of Liberty."

Is famous for coining the first rule of advertising, "Never let the truth get in the way of a good story."

He struggles to think of weird things about himself.

Stan doesn't shake hands, but he will give you a fist bump.

WEIRD THINGS ABOUT DAVID:

He's 6'6" tall...6'9" in heels. His wife is just 5'3."

He has three daughters. He is the only man at his house. Even the dog is a girl.

He was once hit by a truck while running.

He has two screws in his elbow and two screws in his tibia.

He has been in the emergency room 11 times, once in Ukraine.

He has eaten brains in Pakistan, barracuda in Nigeria, and eel in Chile.

His thumb looks like a big toe.

He has Morton's Toe. His second toe is longer than his big toe.

He is not good at lying.

He has not met any women at the baggage claim in Amsterdam.

He loves McDonald's shamrock shakes.

180

STAN PHELPS

Stan Phelps is a best-selling author, keynote speaker, and workshop facilitator. He believes that today's organizations must focus on meaningful differentiation to win the hearts of both employees and customers.

He is the founder of PurpleGoldfish.com. Purple Goldfish is a think tank of customer experience and employee engagement experts that offers keynotes and workshops that drive loyalty and sales. The group helps organizations connect with the hearts and minds of customers and employees.

Prior to PurpleGoldfish.com, Stan had a 20-year career in marketing that included leadership positions at IMG, adidas, PGA Exhibitions, and Synergy. At Synergy, he worked on award-winning experiential programs for top brands such as KFC, Wachovia, NASCAR, Starbucks, and M&M's.

Stan is a TEDx speaker, a *Forbes* contributor, and IBM Futurist. His writing is syndicated on top sites such as Customer Think and Business2Community. He has spoken at over 300 events in Australia, Bahrain, Canada, Ecuador, France, Germany, Holland, Israel, Japan, Malaysia, Peru, Sweden, Russia, Spain, UK, and the U.S.

He is the author of seven other books:

- *Purple Goldfish - 12 Ways to Win Customers and Influence Word of Mouth*
- *Green Goldfish - 15 Ways to Drive Employee Engagement and Reinforce Culture*
- *Golden Goldfish - The Vital Few*
- *Blue Goldfish - Using Technology, Data, and Analytics to Drive Both Profits and Prophets*
- *Purple Goldfish Service Edition - 12 Ways Hotels, Restaurants and Airlines Win the Right Customers*
- *Red Goldfish - Motivating Sales and Loyalty Through Shared Passion and Purpose*
- *Bar Tricks, Bad Jokes, and Even Worse Stories*

Stan received a BS in Marketing and Human Resources from Marist College, a JD/MBA from Villanova University, and a certificate for Achieving Breakthrough Service from Harvard Business School. He is a Certified Net Promoter Associate and has taught as an adjunct professor at NYU, Rutgers University, and Manhattanville College. Stan lives in Cary, North Carolina, with his wife, Jennifer, and two boys, Thomas & James.

Stan is also a fellow at Maddock Douglas, an innovation consulting firm in Chicago.

To book Stan for an upcoming keynote, webinar, or workshop, go stanphelpsspeaks.com. You can reach Stan at stan@purplegoldfish.com or call +1.919.360.4702.

DAVID RENDALL

During the last fifteen years, David Rendall has spoken to audiences on every inhabited continent. His clients include the U.S. Air Force, Australian Government, and Fortune 50 companies such as Microsoft, AT&T, United Health Group, Fannie Mae, and State Farm.

Prior to becoming a speaker, he was a leadership professor and stand-up comedian. He also managed nonprofit enterprises that provided employment for people with disabilities.

In between presentations, David competes in ultramarathons and Ironman triathlons.

David has a doctor of management degree in organizational leadership as well as a graduate degree in psychology. He is the author of four other books:

- *The Four Factors of Effective Leadership*

- *The Freak Factor*

- *The Freak Factor for Kids*

- *21st Century Leadership in the Arab World*

David is also a fellow at Maddock Douglas, an innovation consulting firm in Chicago.

To book David for an upcoming keynote, webinar, or workshop, go drendall.com. You can reach David at dave@drendall.com or call +1.919.222.6295.

ADDITIONAL INSPIRATION AND RECOMMENDED READING

- *Different*, Youngme Moon
- *Blue Ocean Strategy*, W. Chan Kim and Renee Mauborgne
- *Blue Ocean Shift*, W. Chan Kim and Renee Mauborgne
- *Purple Cow*, Seth Godin
- *The Freak Factor*, David Rendall
- *The Power of Moments*, Chip and Dan Heath
- *Made to Stick*, Chip and Dan Heath
- *Stand Out*, Dorie Clark
- *Barking Up the Wrong Tree*, Eric Barker
- *The Power of Small*, Robert Koval and Linda Kaplan Thaler
- *Free the Idea Monkey*, Mike Maddock
- *Uncommon Service*, Frances Frei and Anne Morriss
- *The Gifts of Imperfection*, Brené Brown
- *Becoming a Category of One*, Joe Calloway
- *Contagious*, Jonah Berger
- *Youtility*, Jay Baer

OTHER COLORS IN THE GOLDFISH SERIES

Purple Goldfish – 12 Ways to Win Customers and Influence Word of Mouth. This book is based on the Purple Goldfish Project, a crowdsourcing effort that collected more than 1,001 examples of signature-added value. The book draws inspiration from the concept of lagniappe, providing 12 practical strategies for winning the hearts of customers and influencing positive word of mouth.

Green Goldfish – Beyond Dollars: 15 Ways to Drive Employee Engagement and Reinforce Culture. Green Goldfish examines the importance of employee engagement in today's workplace. The book showcases 15 signature ways to increase employee engagement beyond compensation to reinforce the culture of an organization.

Golden Goldfish – The Vital Few: All Customers and Employees Are Not Created Equal. Golden Goldfish examines the importance of your top 20 percent of customers and employees. The book showcases nine ways to drive loyalty and retention with these two critical groups.

Blue Goldfish - Using Technology, Data, and Analytics to Drive Both Profits and Prophets. Blue Goldfish examines how to leverages technology, data, and analytics to do a "little something extra" to improve the experience for the customer. The book is based on a collection of over 300 case studies. It examines the three R's: Relationship, Responsiveness, and Readiness. Blue Goldfish also uncovers eight different ways to turn insights into action.

Red Goldfish - Motivating Sales and Loyalty Through Shared Passion and Purpose. Purpose is changing the way we work and how customers choose business partners. It is driving loyalty, and it's on its way to becoming the ultimate differentiator in business. *Red Goldfish* shares cutting edge examples and reveals the eight ways businesses can embrace purpose that drives employee engagement, fuels the bottom line, and makes an impact on the lives of those it serves.

Purple Goldfish Service Edition - 12 Ways Hotels, Restaurants, and Airlines Win the Right Customers. *Purple Goldfish Service Edition* is about differentiation via added value. Marketing to your existing customers via G.L.U.E. (giving little unexpected extras). Packed with over 100 examples, the book focuses on the 12 ways to do the "little extras" to improve the customer experience for restaurants, hotels, and airlines. The end result is increased sales, happier customers, and positive word of mouth.

Made in the USA
Lexington, KY
11 September 2018